Praise for
The Seasons of God

"*Never!* Now that's a big statement. However, I have never heard a better Bible teacher than Richard Blackaby. To say that I am excited about this new book is the understatement of the new millennium! Read with anticipation about the seasons of your life and be inspired to make the most of each."

> —JOHNNY HUNT, senior pastor of First Baptist Church,
> Woodstock, GA

"Time is both one of the world's greatest resources and one of the most misused. Blackaby does a masterful job in showing how God has given us seasons of life to make the most of the time we have."

> —WILL GRAHAM, executive director of the Billy Graham
> Training Center

"God has uniquely gifted Richard with the ability to explain life in a way that is fascinating, enjoyable, and always eye-opening. This book will make you think. It will help you see God in everything from your crises to the mundane. Ultimately it will compel you to live your life with renewed fervency and joy."

> —HENRY T. BLACKABY, author of *Experiencing God*

"This book is one of those rare finds. Not only does it bring fresh insight to familiar scriptures, but it is also practical. This is a concept that will immediately change the way you view your circumstances and will help you redefine your outlook. *The Seasons of God* is written out of a deep well of wisdom drawn from experience, by an author willing to be authentic and transparent in his communication."

> —JENNIFER KENNEDY DEAN, author of *Live a Praying Life*
> and executive director of the Praying Life Foundation

"I have worked with Richard Blackaby for a number of years and have been impressed by his ability to use compelling stories and images to communicate profound truths. In this new book he expertly describes how our lives flow through seasons. I am impressed with how Richard explains life in ways you may never have considered before. But most importantly, he demonstrates how you can thrive in every stage of your life. This is one of those books that can change the way you think and live."

—DICK SCHULTZ, executive director of the National Collegiate Athletic Association (ret.) and executive director of the United States Olympic Committee (ret.)

"The ebb and flow of life has a rhythm, best lived in step with God as our Creator and Sustainer. Reading this book will help you find His pace for the current season of your life. God is constant, life is constantly changing, and our perspective on both must continually mature to fully experience His best."

—JEFF IORG, president of Golden Gate Baptist Theological Seminary

"In *The Seasons of God,* you will find yourself understanding in new ways why certain things work the way they do at certain times of life. Read this book slowly and keep it handy, because Blackaby gives a lot of theological, biblical, and practical understanding of how God works in every season. You'll want to refer to it the next time the weather changes in your own life."

—MIKE GLENN, author of *The Gospel of Yes* and senior pastor of Brentwood Baptist Church, Brentwood, TN

"In this helpful work Richard Blackaby coaches us all to see the seasons of our lives from God's perspective and from that vantage point to anticipate the new things He might have in store. Richard draws inspiration and insight from his own personal pilgrimage shaped by the context of

God's living Word to produce a thoughtful blueprint for any stage of life. *The Seasons of God* will be a helpful book for those courageous enough to honestly follow God well in the next chapter of life."

—JEFF CHRISTOPHERSON, vice president of the North
American Mission Board and author of *Kingdom Matrix*

"Sometimes we are so busy living the grind of daily life that we fail to step back and see things from a larger view. Knowing life comes in seasons can help us face those occasional hurricanes that seem to blast us off our path and can help us enjoy the warmth of the good days. Read this book, whatever season you find yourself in. Take time to reflect, to be encouraged, and to press on."

—ALVIN L. REID, professor of evangelism and student
ministry, Bailey Smith Chair of Evangelism,
Southeastern Baptist Theological Seminary

"With humor, wit, and wisdom, Richard Blackaby poses a most important question: Are you thriving or merely surviving in your current season of life? This book is rife with laughter, transparency, and spiritual insights. A refreshing, delightful read that, if taken to heart, could show us how to be truly happy in Jesus."

—CONNIE CAVANAUGH, speaker and author of *From
Faking It to Finding Grace* and *Following God One
Yes at a Time*

"Whether you're in hard times or good, old age or youth, this book is sure to comfort, encourage, and enlighten. It will help you understand where you've been, fully embrace where you are, and prepare you for where you're going. Don't allow another season to race by without experiencing all that God has in store for your life."

—DANIEL BLACKABY, author of *When Worlds Collide*
and *Legend of the Book Keeper*

The SEASONS of GOD

How the Shifting Patterns of Your Life
Reveal His Purposes for You

RICHARD BLACKABY

MULTNOMAH
BOOKS

THE SEASONS OF GOD
PUBLISHED BY MULTNOMAH BOOKS
12265 Oracle Boulevard, Suite 200
Colorado Springs, Colorado 80921

ISBN 978-1-59052-942-3
ISBN 978-1-60142-418-1 (electronic)

Cover design by Kelly L. Howard

Published in association with the literary agency of Wolgemuth & Associates, Inc.

Published in the United States by WaterBrook Multnomah, an imprint of the Crown Publishing Group, a division of Random House Inc., New York.

MULTNOMAH and its mountain colophon are registered trademarks of Random House Inc.

Library of Congress Cataloging-in-Publication Data
Blackaby, Richard, 1961-
    The seasons of God : how the shifting patterns of your life reveal his purposes for you / Richard Blackaby. — 1st ed.
        p. cm.
    Includes bibliographical references.
    ISBN 978-1-59052-942-3 — ISBN 978-1-60142-418-1 (electronic)
    1. Seasons—Religious aspects—Christianity. 2. Christian life. I. Title.
    BV4509.5.B548 2012
    248.4—dc23

                                                    2012020217

Printed in the United States of America
2012—First Edition

10 9 8 7 6 5 4 3 2 1

SPECIAL SALES
Most WaterBrook Multnomah books are available at special quantity discounts when purchased in bulk by corporations, organizations, and special-interest groups. Custom imprinting or excerpting can also be done to fit special needs. For information, please e-mail SpecialMarkets@ WaterBrookMultnomah.com or call 1-800-603-7051.

To my wife, Lisa,
who has made experiencing each new season
a joy and an adventure!

CONTENTS

PART THREE: THRIVING IN ALL OUR SEASONS

ACKNOWLEDGMENTS

Winston Churchill, himself a prolific author, once declared, "Writing a book is an adventure. To begin with, it is a toy and an amusement. Then it becomes a mistress, and then it becomes a master, then a tyrant. The last phase is that just as you are about to be reconciled to your servitude, you kill the monster and fling him out to the public."

This project has provided me a greater appreciation for Churchill's observation. Writing this book required significant thought and reflection, demanding that I look from an entirely new vantage point at a subject I assumed was sublimely familiar. Perhaps the greatest challenge associated with tackling this theme was its broad scope. It's about *life*—from birth to death—and that's a wide swath to cut. The seasons are familiar yet filled with mystery. I assumed I was dealing with the obvious, yet the next moment I uncovered a fresh insight that caught me entirely by surprise. I found that looking at life from a fresh perspective is challenging but also infinitely rewarding, and I trust it will be that way for you also.

Throughout the course of writing, I've been enormously encouraged and ably assisted by numerous talented (and long-suffering) people.

My wife, Lisa, has been my faithful support and inspiration. She has worked tirelessly to add laughter into the life of her hopelessly task-oriented husband. She also has been indentured to me for three decades as my chief editor and supportive critic.

Special thanks also to my beautiful daughter, Carrie. This is the first book to which she has applied her considerable editing skills, and it has given me renewed confidence in what an English degree from college can do.

I'm immensely grateful to Mike and Daniel for allowing me to share their struggles and foibles. They're nothing if not transparent. With them, I don't even have to exaggerate!

Special thanks also to Terry Milne Osgood, who graciously applied her impressive analytical mind to these pages and offered so many insightful comments.

To my parents, who despite numerous adversities and financial challenges, provided me a home that resounded with laughter: Thank you, Mom and Dad. It's been a great journey!

Finally, thanks to Thomas Womack for his considerable and insightful editing skills and to Ken Petersen of WaterBrook Multnomah Publishing Group for his patience and wisdom. It has been my pleasure working with you!

PART ONE

EMBRACING
the PATTERN

1

FINDING OUR BEARINGS

Are you sure you should be reading this book? I mean, right here, right this moment?

Now, to be honest, I'm fairly confident your best answer to that question is yes—maybe even "Yes, *absolutely!*" I asked because, you see, this book explores something that involves getting your *timing* right for all you do and where you do it. It's about being free to really enjoy what you're doing and where you're doing it—and to make the most of every experience.

Let me picture it for you.

HOW DID I GET HERE?

My son Daniel has given our family numerous reasons to chuckle. Often he makes us laugh so hard our sides hurt. He's that kind of guy.

For instance, there was that time in Hawaii. I'd been the president of a graduate school in Canada for ten years when the board of trustees surprised me. Wanting to thank me for the school's progress, they voted to send my wife and me to Hawaii. Living in Alberta, we faced January temperatures plunging to minus-forty degrees, so we enthusiastically accepted the board's generous expression of appreciation.

My three teenage children soon approached me with a grave concern. They feared we couldn't possibly enjoy ourselves all alone in the tropics, knowing that they were shivering back home in the Arctic air, parentless.

The next thing I knew, they were coming too, and our all-expenses-paid, romantic getaway became an exorbitant family odyssey.

The day we flew out of Calgary, the mercury was sitting at minus twenty-eight. Long hours later upon landing in Lihue, Kauai, we were greeted by temperatures in the seventies. We rented a car and drove to our lodging. In under a minute our pale-skinned, sun-starved offspring dashed into our beachfront town house and emerged in their swimming attire, ready for action. With nary a comment such as "Dad, is there anything we can do to help?" they sprinted to the beach.

Jet-lagged and famished, I found the nearest grocery store and stocked up on essential food supplies, including copious amounts of snacks for my freeloading teens. Lisa began nesting—sorting the bedding and assigning rooms.

Finally my wife and I trudged wearily to the beach. Daniel greeted us cheerfully. "Did you get any good food? I'm starving!" I hastily assured him I had no intention of making him lunch but that the patio door to our town house was unlocked and there was now a plethora of overpriced groceries awaiting him.

He meandered back to the town house and discovered, much to his delight, a bountiful supply of all his favorite junk food—Double Stuf Oreo cookies, nacho chips, and plenty more. He voraciously ripped open a bag of cookies and popped the tab on a can of Coke.

Flopping happily onto the couch in his soaking-wet swimsuit, my son parked his sand-covered feet on the coffee table. Spewing all manner of crumbs and debris as he inhaled his snacks, he flipped on the television and... *Could it be? ESPN? A hockey game?* Life did not get any better!

He sighed in contentment and surveyed his surroundings. To his right he could see ocean waves lazily rolling in. In his lap lay the food of the gods. Before him a large-screen TV featured his most beloved sport.

And emerging to his left—a scowling stranger clad in only a towel.

It was at that precise moment Daniel realized *he was in the wrong town house!*

"How did I get here?" our embarrassed son wondered on that lazy, tropical day. He'd been minding his own business, enjoying what life placed before him, and simply trying to satisfy his appetite.

Now, in and of itself, that particular town house was by no means an inappropriate environment for Daniel. And it's easy to imagine a situation in which nothing at all would be wrong about his being there. As a fun-to-have-around guy, Daniel might have eventually met that stranger's family on the beach and received an invitation to drop by (along with his parents and siblings, I like to think). Or, on a repeat vacation to Hawaii (one can hope!), that town house might actually become the one rented by our family.

But on that particular day, those were *not* the governing circumstances. And so, to his horror, Daniel discovered that he wasn't where he thought he was or wanted to be—and he certainly wasn't wanted where he was!

Life can be like that sometimes. We can get our bearings confused and misunderstand the cues coming from our environment.

THE ISSUE

For Daniel, his misunderstanding resulted in his having to bolt out a patio door in serpentine fashion, mumbling apologies along the way. But for the larger and more profound misunderstanding that pertains to this book's topic, the consequences can be tragic.

It's an oversight that can fill our outlook on life with confusion, doubt, and stress. *How did this happen?* we end up asking ourselves. *Why*

am I here? What brought me to this point? Am I stuck in this mess forever?
Our situation seems so far from what we planned, what we expected,
what we hoped. How did all that slip away?

Relationships, jobs, and opportunities that began with such promise
can degenerate into lethargy, disappointment, regret, and even bitterness.

Ultimately, this huge misconception I'm speaking of can lead to
wasted months, lost years—even a squandered life.

It can play out like this:

- A young husband and wife grow disillusioned about their
  marriage; their bliss once held eternal promise but now seems
  crushed under the suffocating weight of unmet expectations.
- A mother and father are bewildered by their adolescent son's
  anger and rebellion; the child they loved as a preschooler,
  who gave them so much love and joy in return, has become
  a stranger.
- A woman in her fifties wrestles with the depressing awareness
  that certain dreams, cherished since her youth, may never
  find fulfillment.
- A man in his thirties languishes in a difficult job, but the
  worst struggle of all happens every morning as he searches for
  a compelling motivation to embrace the day.
- An executive who has achieved tremendous success in his
  career now reaches the sickening realization that his ambition
  cost him his family.
- A talented and personable young woman who once enjoyed
  setting enthusiastic goals for herself now finds that she's bored
  with life.

How do we prevent those scenarios?

Can they be avoided?

An invaluable part of the answer is to better recognize the proper
flow of our lives from God's perspective—and, in particular, to catch the

God-designed seasonal rhythms that underlie His plans for us, in everything we do.

TOTAL COVERAGE

Probably the most famous Scripture passage that addresses this issue is found in Ecclesiastes 3, beginning with the well-known words "To everything there is a *season,* a *time* for every purpose under heaven." This and the following lines are a favorite passage for many, filled with that attractive mix of the familiar and the mysterious that so often gives memorable poetry its greatness and power.

To step back a little for a bigger view, you may recall how the book of Ecclesiastes paints a broad-stroke portrait of "everything that is done *under the sun*" (1:14, ESV)—that is, of life's reality as considered especially from a this-world, here-and-now perspective.

I'm sure you also remember from the creation account in Genesis 1 that the sun is described there as the "greater light" among the heavenly beacons God created as markers "for signs and *seasons,* and for days and years" (verses 14, 16). So as far back as the opening page of Scripture, we see the *seasons* as a dynamic, God-ordained feature of life on earth.

This leads us to something we learned in science class at school—how the earth's tilt on its axis is what allows the sun's influence to bring about the seasons we experience. During our planet's yearly orbit around the sun, the Northern Hemisphere warms up as it swings around and faces the sun more directly (reaching a peak in June); six months later it's the Southern Hemisphere's turn to do the same, leaving the northern regions to chill.

Maybe you've wondered about this. Exactly *why* did the Creator set it up this way and divide the year into seasons? Since the Bible emphasizes that God made the earth "good" (as we're told seven times in Genesis 1), why didn't He simply set the earth's thermostat to a comfortable room temperature and create a greenhouse effect year round? Why include dramatic climatic changes throughout each year, from bitter cold in the dead of winter to sweltering heat during summer? As a dad who's bankrolling a fashion-conscious daughter, I'm fully aware of the expense of maintaining separate wardrobes to accommodate four rotating seasons!

Of course, not every region of the world has four clearly distinct seasons. The Arctic and Antarctica never warm up because their latitudes are too extreme; seasons there are identified by the amount of sunlight they receive, or the lack thereof. In regions closest to the equator, where the earth's tilt is hardly noticeable, temperatures stay fairly constant, and seasons are more typically thought of as wet or dry (though even these rainfall patterns are ultimately affected by the sun's influence and the earth's tilt).

Moreover, because oceans warm up and cool off at different rates than dry land does, islands and coastal regions tend to have much more moderate seasonal changes than inland areas do. Related to this is the fact that the Northern Hemisphere has larger land masses than the Southern Hemisphere has, bringing differences in how the seasons are experienced in the north and the south. (All of which means…if you're reading this while living in a South Atlantic beach house near the tip of Argentina, you might have to take my word for some things.)

By now I've taxed the limits of my scientific pedagogical abilities. (I passed high school physics only because I was astute enough to recruit a brilliant lab partner.) My overall point here is simply this: God intentionally, right from the start, built change and variety into creation, and the upshot for you and me is that *things don't stay the same.* God loves order, but He also delights in diversity; He therefore combined the two when He created the earth.

And so, when we push farther into the Bible and reach Ecclesiastes, where we come across that repeated phrase "under the sun," we already have an awareness of these God-designed, sun-triggered seasonal features in the background of our existence.

Easily Forgotten

Let's focus again on that evocative passage in Ecclesiastes 3, beginning with the first eight verses. Read these lines carefully:

To everything there is a season,
A time for every purpose under heaven:

A time to be born,
    And a time to die;
A time to plant,
    And a time to pluck what is planted;
A time to kill,
    And a time to heal;
A time to break down,
    And a time to build up;
A time to weep,
    And a time to laugh;
A time to mourn,
    And a time to dance;
A time to cast away stones,
    And a time to gather stones;
A time to embrace,
    And a time to refrain from embracing;
A time to gain,
    And a time to lose;
A time to keep,
    And a time to throw away;
A time to tear,
    And a time to sew;
A time to keep silence,
    And a time to speak;

A time to love,
   And a time to hate;
A time of war,
   And a time of peace. (3:1–8)

On the face of it, the passage seems pretty straightforward: at various points in time, different stuff happens. *Of course. So what?*

Or, if you're in a gloomier frame of mind, you might be tempted to see here "the tyranny of time," as one Old Testament scholar describes it:

We throw ourselves into some absorbing activity which offers us fulfillment, but how freely did we choose it? How soon shall we be doing the exact opposite? Perhaps our choices are no freer than our responses to winter and summer, childhood and old age, dictated by the march of time and of unbidden change. Looked at this way, the repetition of "a time...and a time..." begins to be oppressive.[1]

But few of us, I suspect, respond to these lines that way, especially when we apply some sensitive reflection. In fact, as simple as the subject may seem on the surface, for thousands of years this passage has captivated human hearts. And it continues to do so because its message is, in reality, deeply profound. Our hearts instantly perceive (perhaps subconsciously) that this is a message we all too easily lose touch with. Here's something we know in the core of our being to be essentially true, a precious certainty, yet we forget it oh so quickly, to our detriment.

That message is stated straightforwardly in the opening lines: everything in our lives has a season, an appropriate time—not in some random way but in a manner that's charged with purpose. Which means we're to recognize "human experience as a tapestry woven of 'times,'" as another Bible scholar expresses it.[2]

To further impress the message on our hearts and minds and to help us realize how it covers life's totality, the author of Ecclesiastes goes on to express our human activities and experiences in fourteen contrasting pairs (that's twice times seven—the Bible's symbolic number for perfection or completion).[3]

The expressions appear to mix both literal and metaphorical meanings. Birth and death, weeping and laughing, mourning and dancing—these seem clear enough. "A time to break down, and a time to build up" can easily remind us that "there are simply times in life for construction and times for dismantling"[4] in a variety of endeavors.

A few expressions in the passage are more obscure to us today, like "a time to cast away stones, and a time to gather stones" (3:5). The Hebrew word here for "stone" can be used for precious stones, so it's possible that this phrase "concerns the accumulation and distribution of wealth."[5] It could have the general meaning that there are times in life when we gather and other times when we disperse. Following up on that, the focus of the next line—"a time to embrace, and a time to refrain from embracing"—"may well allude to the embracing of wealth." This in turn might carry over to what comes next: "a time to gain, and a time to lose" may represent "the acquisitive search for wealth and its loss"—with the thought then completed in the next line: "a time to keep, and a time to throw away."[6]

That interpretation is reinforced by the strong and clear cautions against materialistic "gain" or "profit" that we read throughout Ecclesiastes (as in 1:3; 2:11; and 5:16). And it's brought up here in chapter 3 in the verse that immediately follows our list of fourteen pairs: "What profit has the worker from that in which he labors?" (verse 9). Apparently one thing the author of Ecclesiastes strongly wants us to grasp from this list is that a seasonal perspective on life helps us guard against the kind of existence that becomes consumed with amassing possessions and wealth. That's reason enough to start thinking more seasonally!

Meanwhile the lines that come later in the list appear to focus more on relationships—our conversations, loving and hating, conflict and peace. (Even "a time to tear, and a time to sew" may serve as a picture of breaking off or mending relationships.) Our friendships and other personal associations and even the things we say to one another—all of it, like all of life, is intended to be seen in light of seasonal considerations.

AND IT'S BEAUTIFUL!

Reinforcing his message, the author of Ecclesiastes goes on to tell us this about God: "He has made everything beautiful *in its time*" (3:11). Our ability to taste life's experiences *at their best* is governed by their seasonality. At the right time they're not just pleasant or convenient but something far better; they're actually *beautiful*—beautifully appropriate, beautifully satisfying for us. A perfect fit!

This passage helps us "to see perpetual change not as something unsettling but as an unfolding pattern, scintillating and God-given." We might suppose we'd prefer a permanently stable life with fixed and comfortable routines, but "there is something better.… Instead of frozen perfection there is the kaleidoscopic movement of innumerable processes, each with its own character and period of blossoming and ripening, beautiful in its time and contributing to the over-all masterpiece which is the work of one Creator."[7]

We're all capable—to some degree, at least—of appreciating this seasonally unfolding beauty because of something else God has done, which this same verse declares: "He has put eternity in their hearts, except that no one can find out the work that God does from beginning to end" (3:11). The eternity in our hearts lets us start glimpsing here and now the perspective we'll gain to the full only when we have the vantage point of heaven.

But the point is, we *can* start grasping it now. And that makes all the difference in the world.

It enables us to do what Ecclesiastes 3 immediately instructs its readers to do: "to *rejoice,* and to *do good* in their lives, and also that every man should eat and drink and *enjoy* the good of all his labor—it is the gift of God" (verses 12–13). The Bible intends for people to live life with gusto!

THE SEASONAL ULTIMATE

There's a great deal more in this third chapter of Ecclesiastes that's well worth our attention, but let's consider just one thing further. The seasonal theme will be repeated once more in this chapter, this time in the context of *the* most important issues of our lives—sin and judgment and ultimately our salvation in Christ.

The author of Ecclesiastes looked around him at situations where justice and righteousness should be evident, only to observe that "wickedness was there" and "iniquity was there" (verse 16). Maybe he was thinking about courtrooms, government halls, and the marketplace, or maybe he thought primarily of the human heart. Or all the above. Evil was everywhere.

But he did not despair over this; he went on: "I said in my heart, 'God shall judge the righteous and the wicked, for *there is a time...for every purpose and for every work*'" (verse 17). Even when injustice and corruption appear unhindered in their pollution, a seasonal perspective enables us to hold on to God's hope. He *will,* in His perfect timing, make things right—preparing the way for the triumph of every good purpose and every good work.

The believer in Christ knows something here that Old Testament saints could glimpse only faintly: the ultimate good purposes and good works mentioned here will find their glorious fulfillment in Jesus and His gospel.

Even that was profoundly a matter of correct timing. It's "when the fullness of the time had come" that God sent Jesus into our world (Galatians 4:4)—this Jesus who came to die for us "at the right time" (Romans 5:6, ESV).

THE FULL SCOPE

This brings us to a sweeping conclusion: every aspect of our lives is governed by the ebb and flow of seasons.

That's why the truths you'll find in this book are so important. In the following pages you may gain an entirely new, fresh, and exciting way to view and understand your life.

As the chapters unfold, we'll take a look at "Ten Laws of the Seasons of Life" (chapter 3). We'll examine the particular benefits you can gain from sharpening your seasonal antenna ("Benefits of a Seasonal Perspective," chapter 4). We'll look at specific arenas of life where the seasonal perspective is especially important ("Strengthening Your Seasonal Perspective," chapter 5). Then we'll begin surveying, one by one, each of the four different seasons and see how they uniquely affect you and what promises they hold for you in each phase of your life.

*But first...*to help you gain a better feel for an outlook on life that may initially seem strange to you, join me in a brief retro journey through some seasons I've passed through.

REFLECT AND RESPOND

1. On a scale of one to ten, how highly would you rate your satisfaction with your life right now? What would it take to elevate your living to a higher level? What is preventing you from doing that?

2. What is your favorite season in nature? Why is that?

3. Why do you think God delights so much in diversity—as reflected in the earth's seasonal changes as well as in many other aspects of creation? Does your life reflect the diversity and change God built into nature?

4. Look back at Ecclesiastes 3:1–8. Which phrase best describes where your life is right now?

5. As you reflect on the biblical principle that everything in life has a season, an appropriate time, to what extent do you think you consciously apply that principle to your daily activities and decisions? What do you think could help you become better at maximizing each season in your life?

2

MAKING THE ROUNDS

I had a friend who liked to begin his speeches by saying, "I was born at a young age..." (It seemed funny at the time.)

I, like everyone else, began life as a child. In fact, I did so in more ways than one.

BACKYARD MASTER

Every cycle and every stage of life begins with spring—and the first spring of my life occurred at my birth. *Everything* was new! I hadn't even met my parents before. Every sight, sound, smell, and touch was invigorating.

I eventually advanced into the summer season of my preschool years. I grew like a weed and became stronger. I learned to walk and run and talk. Could I ever talk!

By the time I turned five, I was in my autumn as a preschooler. I lived in a quaint suburban home in Southern California, and I was the master of our beautiful backyard. It had seemed so enormous and mysterious to me when I first ventured into it. It was expansive enough to embrace several locales, including a garden area and a fishpond. In time, after extensive exploration and endless playing, I was perfectly comfortable leading my younger brothers through the grounds on safaris, or in a posse pursuing bad guys, or in a heroic quest through a dark forest inhabited by monsters.

By then I was in my prime as a preschooler. I knew what to expect. I had my routine (including the dreaded afternoon nap).

Then something terrible happened. My entire world was torn asunder. A cold, dark winter set in. I was exiled to kindergarten. I exited my preschool stage and entered a new springtime as I commenced my elementary school stage of life.

As a five-year-old, I'd been at the top of my game. As the oldest of my siblings, I was the strongest, smartest, fastest, and most experienced preschooler on the premises, and I was used to having my peers look up to me with reverential awe.

But it had all been temporary.

Gone were the carefree days of having few decisions beyond which game to play next and how to make myself scarce when my mother announced it was nap time. Now each morning while my younger brothers pulled out their toys for another day of adventure, I was scrubbed, dressed, and dispatched to a strange place.

Drastic Measures

The spring season of my elementary school years encompassed a bundle of conflicting emotions. It was strangely exhilarating to face such an enormous new challenge. I sensed a huge, new world opening before me, but at first I was extremely intimidated.

Just getting to school involved a measure of trepidation. My mother drove me there, and the route led past a large high school that looked like a massive fortress among the orange trees, occupied by giant mutants. Those swarming battalions of monstrous teenagers terrified me! I felt like an unarmed dwarf, and the feeling persisted even in my own classroom surrounded by human beings of "normal" dimensions like my own.

At home I'd been extroverted and outspoken, confident in my abilities and knowledge. Not anymore. My road to restored confidence was impeded by many a sore trial.

I remember arriving at school one day only to make a horrific discovery. In my pocket was my beloved pirate pistol (previously used by Blackbeard, I believed). I'd used it earlier that morning in an epic battle with my brothers. For the first time in my life, it dawned on me that perhaps not everyone carried firearms in their pockets. What if people saw my gun and...*laughed* at me?

As a five-year-old, I was struck—as most novice students eventually are—with the reality that I might be ridiculed at school for something I took for granted at home. I realized my comfortable preschool world was clashing with the cruel elementary school world.

I dreaded being discovered in class with a toy weapon. I imagined my sinister kindergarten teacher triumphantly confiscating it and making me walk the plank in front of all the other children.

I was reduced to drastic measures.

I found a patch of tall grass by the fence surrounding the school and carefully concealed my weapon. It was my most prized possession, but I dared not risk having anyone find it on my person.

As soon as school was over, I dashed back to recover my hidden treasure, but it was gone. I never saw it again.

I still miss that gun.

Mercifully, fortune eventually shone upon me in elementary school. One by one I made some friends. After all these years I still remember John and Neil and others who became my constant companions. After a few near catastrophes, including almost flunking kindergarten and being erroneously diagnosed with a brain tumor (my brothers like to note that doctors finally took x-rays of my brain but found nothing), I experienced moderate academic success.

Eventually I entered my summer season as an elementary student, a period characterized by growth and maturity. I tried my hand at sports. I ventured to develop more friendships and to hone my skills at school as well as on the playground.

By the time I reached the seventh grade, I was in autumn. I entered some advanced classes and was one of the better players on my soccer and basketball teams. I began to understand my developing identity, and I discovered my niche in certain school subjects and sports. It had been a long journey since I'd fearfully entered kindergarten, but I had finally made it back to the top of my game.

Then winter set in, again. I entered my teen years. My peers were changing—many, it seemed, for the worse. Some of my friends were discarding the innocent games of childhood for depraved fixations of adolescence. A few were eagerly taking teenage crudeness and profanity to shockingly low levels.

We all knew the end of an era had come. By the time we reached the eighth grade, we were the biggest kids on the playground. Many of my classmates had known one another for most of their lives. But after a largely forgettable graduation evening, each of us left that school for the final time and began a new spring season—in high school.

More to Learn

I remember my first week in high school. I was a skinny, apprehensive fourteen-year-old with braces. One day I was late leaving school and was forced to walk past the senior football team as they were preparing to take the field for practice. One of the linemen grabbed me as I timidly tried to sneak by. He decided to use my face to test the firmness of his new shoulder pads. Thankfully his pads managed to withstand the impact of my face, but my braces snagged his jersey. When he shoved me away from him, threads from his uniform caught in my braces and began unraveling.

He was not amused.

How does a fearful freshman respond rationally when a senior football player angrily accuses him of damaging his jersey with his face?

In that moment I had an epiphany: I clearly saw that I was no longer at the top of the school food chain. I'd entered a new spring season in my life, and in many ways it would be wildly different than the springs I'd experienced in my preschool days or in elementary school.

Once again I commenced this new stage of life with a blend of trepidation and excitement (after I learned to use a different exit than the one used by the football team). So many experiences were new and challenging for me. I'd never had a locker before. Everyone seemed much bigger and older. Some already had adult bodies. I was too intimidated to try out for the freshman basketball team until a friend insisted I should.

Gradually I once again discovered fields in which I excelled (basketball, soccer, social studies) and fields in which I did not (French, algebra, chemistry… Did I mention French?).

By my senior year I finally hit my stride. I was somewhat popular (if the fact that everyone, including the teachers, called me Beaner has any significance). Having survived my initial run-in with the senior football team, I was now big enough that no one used me for tackle practice.

But as every high school graduate learns, the "real" world awaits those idealistic teenagers excitedly preparing for prom. After four years winter caught up with my life once again. A new spring was waiting in the wings—a massive university. And it didn't even have lockers.

LEAPING ALONG

I'll never forget my first day of university. Since I had been born at the peak of the baby boom, my classes throughout my educational odyssey continually set records for their large size. University was no exception. Schools were desperately pulling professors out of retirement and enlisting graduate students to teach introductory classes to the hordes of freshmen swarming to college the year I arrived.

I have no idea what came over me as I entered the Arts and Sciences Building. I headed up the two-stage ramp leading to the second story, where my Introduction to English class awaited. Suddenly I made a silly, impulse decision. Instead of walking up the first half of the ramp, turning 180 degrees, and continuing up the second half, I decided to leap over the railing partway up and save myself a few steps.

Had the upper ramp been vacant, it might not have been such a bad idea. However, it teemed with people making their way to class.

I took two giant strides, grabbed the handrail to my right, flung my feet high over the railing, and smashed into something with a loud *thump*. That something was an elderly woman, who went crashing to the floor from the force of two size 12 leviathans striking her a near-fatal blow. Her handful of papers fluttered around us like a swarm of angry bats.

I awkwardly offered to assist her to her feet and retrieve her papers, but she angrily dismissed me. I thought it best to be on my way.

Upon reaching my classroom, I spied a high school friend. Things were looking up! Then I noticed my disheveled, elderly acquaintance wandering past the open doorway with a bewildered look on her face. I felt terrible. What if she was wandering aimlessly down the crowded hallways in a daze because of our collision? I felt guilty for not helping her, but I knew she would have none of it.

Then I spied her walking past the door, heading in the opposite direction. Again I felt horrible.

She reappeared a third time—and peered into my classroom. Oh no! What if she was an elderly student and I had to sit beside her the entire semester?

She carefully snaked her way through the rows of desks…and up to the lectern! To my unmitigated horror, she announced she would be our professor for the next four months. (Lord, have mercy!) Any thoughts of my earning an English degree quickly evaporated.

Thus the spring of my college years was ignominiously launched.

I won't take time to walk in detail through all the seasons I've traversed so far. But you see the pattern.

I did make it through university, and upon graduation I got married, moved to Texas, spent seven years in graduate school, and had two kids. More new stages of life were launched. (And I thought high school was challenging!)

Eventually I entered the career stage of life and took my first job as the minister of a local church. (Meanwhile my wife and I had another child, for good measure.) This was my first full-time job in the field of my chosen career. It was exhilarating, challenging, frustrating, and infinitely rewarding. I experienced all four seasons in that position—and eventually came to realize that it was time to move on.

A fresh challenge awaited me that would call upon everything I'd learned thus far in life. A theological seminary asked me to serve as its president. I was only thirty-one. Many people thought I was too young for the job (they were probably right). For the next thirteen years, I grew in that position, progressing from spring to summer to fall and ultimately to winter—and on to a different job. (I'll share more about that in later pages.)

Perhaps I'm an oddity, but in each job I assume I'll retire in it, so I jump in like there is no tomorrow. Inevitably, however, another winter sets in, and I experience closure before a brand-new spring—a new tomorrow—emerges. Seasons in our lives work that way, in all the various aspects of our existence.

You've probably already recognized and picked up from my brief story certain principles about the seasons of life. But let's look at these now with greater focus.

REFLECT AND RESPOND

1. Which stage of your life so far has been the most enjoyable? Why do you think that is?

2. What are some of the seasons you can detect by looking back on your own childhood and youth?

3. What have been the dominant feelings you experienced in the spring, summer, fall, and winter seasons of your life? Does each season bring out different emotions in you?

4. What were some of the biggest challenges you faced in your past as you transitioned from season to season or from one stage of life to the next?

3

TEN LAWS OF THE SEASONS OF LIFE

The key to getting the most out of life—to experiencing everything God intends for us—is found in our *perspective*. A seasonal outlook plays an especially big role in that. It provides a vantage point that allows us to wisely handle expectations, ambitions, and disappointments as well as decision making. It helps us make sense of where we are in life right now…and to be more deliberate about our future.

In the chapters to come, I'll demonstrate just how practical and relevant this seasonal perspective really is. Meanwhile let's explore some of the most basic truths about how life flows in seasons.

1. Each of us experiences repeated cycles in life that are profoundly mirrored in the seasons we see in nature.

The seasons we go through are constantly recurring. All of life is filled with these seasonal rhythms.

Spring is the time of beginnings, exciting opportunities, and anticipation for the future. Seeds planted in this time will then take root and mature during summer's labor, producing a harvest in the fall, a reaping of our efforts. Then everything draws to a close in winter.

2. These seasons are more than simply a metaphor for aging.

The seasonal reality we're exploring in this book is different from merely growing older.

We normally think of childhood and youth as springtime, while summer represents the emerging prime of life. Then autumn starts somewhere beyond middle age perhaps, and everything slows and fades to a finish in elderly wintertime. This is, of course, the overarching seasonal metaphor for life—a true and valid picture.

However, for the seasonal perspective we're looking at here, the driving fundamental is not the concept of our aging but rather our *growth,* our *progress,* our *advancement*—amid a constantly changing environment. As Chili Davis quipped, "Growing old is mandatory; growing up is optional." Understanding our various seasons and making the most of them allows us to keep "growing up" while we're also getting older.

We're aware of our advance through particular *stages* in life—preschool, childhood, youth, college, young adult, middle age, senior adult. What's less evident is that every stage is itself divided into spring, summer, fall, and winter *seasons.*

In each stage of our lives, we'll cycle through spring, summer, autumn, and winter.

3. Each season is unique and adds important dimensions to life.

These seasonal cycles are not haphazard but purposeful—with each season having its own purpose.

Spring is about potential, promise, and possibilities. It's when seeds are planted that later emerge full grown and produce a harvest. It's a time of beginnings. Spring can be invigorating. Whether we're entering a different stage of schooling, launching a new career, or becoming a first-time parent or grandparent, there are certain identifiable moments that usher us into a new stage of life. We won't always be first-year students or entry-level employees or parents of infants, but when we enter those stages of life, spring offers us brand-new opportunities and possibilities. Spring is about *beginnings.*

Summer is a time of growth and maturation. The seeds we planted during spring mature into full-sized plants in the warmth of summer. Summer is when children grow and mature. It's when apprentices develop into skilled craftsmen. For parents it's the "minivan" stage of life when we must shuttle our children between lessons, games, school events, and medical appointments. Summer is the season of *work,* when we invest the time and effort required to become good at what we do.

Autumn is the season of *harvest.* After seeds have been sown, plants have matured, and fruit ripened, autumn produces the reward of our labors. It's when we achieve management positions at work or when we're enlisted to lead and lend advice to various groups in our church and community. It's when we achieve seniority, when we're elected captain of the team or CEO of the company, when we can host a large dinner party with ease, or when our children reach adulthood and become more independent. It's the season when we reach the apex of a particular stage of life. We may not all achieve management positions, but we'll eventually reach the peak of our skills and knowledge in our particular domain. It's when all our music lessons, sports practices, cooking experiments, hours of study, sacrifices made as parents, lessons learned from our failures and successes, and extra effort come to fruition—and we reach the point where we're the leaders and experts in our field. We may not be *the* best in our field, but we're now *our* best.

Winter is a season of winding down—withdrawal, retreat, and closure. Activities, responsibilities, and relationships draw to a close in winter. This is the time of *endings.* It's also a period of rest, restoration, and reflection. It can be a time of solitude. Before you enter your next spring, you must first navigate winter. However, once winter passes, another spring is at the doorstep!

You may be enduring a particularly harsh winter season right now. Perhaps some important responsibilities or relationships have come to an end. You may be wondering what's next. Have no fear! In God's divine plan, even when you're experiencing the bitterest winter of your life, there's another spring on the horizon.

We'll talk in more detail about each season in subsequent chapters, but for now it's important to note that each season is distinct and vitally important for our well-being and success as people.

We often long to reach plateaus, to feel that we've arrived, to settle in and settle down. But our heavenly Father is the God of newness, who makes announcements like these: "Behold, I make *all things new*" (Revelation 21:5). "Behold, the former things have come to pass, and new things I declare; before they spring forth I tell you of them" (Isaiah 42:9). "Behold, I will do a new thing, now it shall spring forth; shall you not know it?" (Isaiah 43:19). Newness is God's specialty, a trademark of the abundant gifts He gives us—and as we traverse the unique succession of seasons He's designed for us, we'll find our way marked by fresh adventures, surprising encounters, and unprecedented fulfillment.

4. Our seasons follow a set order.

This fact may seem blatantly obvious, but it has profound implications. As in nature, the seasons of life progress through a particular sequence. Spring always precedes summer, winter always follows autumn. The pattern stays constant.

Sometimes, in various undertakings, people want to jump straight from the idealistic stage of spring to the harvest season of autumn without putting in the hard work of summer. These people hate practice but want the starring role. They seek a management position at Starbucks before they've proven they can make a good latte.

Likewise, some people avoid winter like the plague. They're slaves to their routines or habits or memories, unwilling to let go of their present way of life so they can experience something new in its place.

The reality is that there's no way to enjoy a new spring if you haven't first journeyed through winter. God designed the order of the seasons, and only He can alter them. Those who try to circumvent the divinely ordained pattern of life are destined for frustration and disappointment.

It's true that occasionally in Scripture we see the seasons described in two divisions rather than four. For example, in one of the promises God gave Noah after the flood, the lasting reality of the seasons (and more) is ensured with these words:

> While the earth remains,
> Seedtime and harvest,
> Cold and heat,
> Winter and summer,
> And day and night
> Shall not cease. (Genesis 8:22)

Now and then in life we might appropriately view a seasonal cycle in two parts rather than four—the opening and the closing, the gearing up and the gearing down. Or occasionally we might identify three simple stages: beginning, middle, and end. But the basic principle of a specific *progression* is always there: the start-up always precedes the close; the seeds are first planted, then they grow, then their fruit is harvested, then the plant dies or becomes dormant, and then a new spring emerges.

In our various endeavors of life, the seasonal transitions can blur at times. One season will often merge and blend into the next rather than occurring with a clear and distinct break from one to the next. But the point is, these transitions *do* occur, one way or another, in an inevitable forward march.

5. Our seasons vary in length and intensity—and in what they require from us.

Talking about weather patterns, we'll sometimes speak of a "short spring" or a "hard winter." Such variations in length and intensity are also true of our seasons of life.

And this is where it can get complicated. Because here's another fact that must be mentioned: seasons have a dark side.

I realized this stark reality last spring. On a beautiful April morning in South Carolina, I went out to my front yard to do some work. A particularly hot, dry summer the previous year had left some barren patches in the lawn. Although not known for my horticultural skills, I'd attempted to patch up the areas with some topsoil and all-purpose grass seed. To my amazement, tiny, slender shoots of grass were tentatively pushing out of the soil skyward. I celebrated my success with a cold glass of iced tea.

Later I learned that at the same time I was pampering the barren spaces on my front lawn, a horrific tornado was striking Alabama and several other Southern states, killing 337 people. While I was fussing over grass shoots, people were dying by the hundreds just two states away as spring tornadoes ripped through their towns and obliterated their homes.

Who experienced spring that day? We all did. There are many endearing aspects of spring, including warm breezes, blossoms, new growth, and fresh, green leaves emerging upon barren branches. But spring holds its dangers as well, including tornadoes and devastating floods. The same season that can bring delight to some can be lethal to others.

That is true of every season. Summer is a time of warmth and growth, but it can also bring scorching heat, drought, and droves of insects. We can get hurricanes in the fall and blizzards in winter.

Likewise, any season in life can bring us ordeals as well as pleasures— and all in an unpredictable array.

Spring is the season of new beginnings, and we're usually imbued with hope as we embark on new ventures. But we can also feel overwhelmed as we face new challenges for which we fear we are ill-equipped.

The first couple of springs in my son Daniel's life were difficult. His first spring set the stage. He was born one month early and was rushed straight into an incubator. As a result, he suffered respiratory problems as a child. The spring of his elementary schooling didn't fare much better. He was a shy child who was mortified to learn that show and tell was mandatory. I received a call at the office asking me to please come to the school immediately. My distraught son was curled up under his desk, refusing to come out.

Daniel began high school suffering from chronic insomnia, apparently untreatable. That led us to homeschool him in an effort to help him obtain both rest and enough academic credits to graduate.

Daniel's entry into college was similarly tumultuous, marred by a first-year English professor who we suspect was an escaped war criminal, judging by her reaction to Daniel's unfortunate propensity for skipping classes.

So you can imagine our mixed emotions as Daniel graduated from college and entered his next spring season by getting married, moving across the country to San Francisco, and entering graduate school. Would this new spring be as bumpy as his previous ones?

To our relief, Daniel blossomed in this new spring season. Not only did he thrive in his marriage to our delightful daughter-in-law Sarah, he also excelled in his master's program (notwithstanding taking Hebrew his first semester). In fact, during his first semester in grad school he started looking at PhD programs (the same child who staged a boycott of show and tell!).

On top of all that, he had his first book published, *When Worlds Collide: Stepping Up and Standing Out in an Anti-God Culture,* coauthored with his brother, Mike. And at the close of his first year of marriage, he signed a contract to publish a fantasy trilogy.

What a relief to know that having to endure a harsh spring (or any other season) in your life doesn't mean that your next time through that season will be equally as difficult.

Conversely, experiencing an enjoyable spring (or fall or winter) doesn't guarantee the next one will be as pleasant.

For one acquaintance of mine, everything seemed to come easily during his early years. Big for his age, this young guy excelled in sports at every level and easily assumed leadership roles. As a star athlete in high school, he was popular with girls and encouraged by teachers. Upon graduation, he was awarded a sports scholarship by the local university. A future in professional sports loomed, and his life appeared to be on the fast track to success.

The previous autumns of this young man's life had always come easily. Due to his size, confidence, and skill, he reaped bountiful harvests following minimal effort in summer.

Then things went terribly wrong.

Touted as an up-and-coming star athlete, this young man was feted by school officials and invited to numerous social events. He partied with abandon while treating his studies with smug disdain. Then his nightmare began. He broke his leg in practice, and his season ended abruptly. Unable to play sports, he had more time to party. With no greater purpose to his life, his socializing led to addiction, failure, and dismissal from college. The harvest from his college labors added up to failure, rejection, and addiction. Life wasn't as easy as it had been during previous autumns.

It's life's diversity that makes it so interesting. The seasons change. Spring flows into summer, then fall, then winter, then spring once again. But the next time around, the seasons may be vastly different. You never know what you'll experience.

Furthermore, your springs will never be identical to those that other people experience. You may have been born into the gentle, warm spring sunlight of a loving home where you were doted upon by both your parents and encouraged to freely explore the world around you. Your friend, meanwhile, may have been reared in an abusive and neglectful environment in which the equivalent of spring tornadoes and floods raged all around him.

Or perhaps your friend began her career with a cutting-edge company led by an enlightened boss who encouraged her to succeed. You, meanwhile, started your career at a struggling company led by an insecure boss who was determined to blame everyone else for his shortcomings.

Plenty of situations we face during life's seasons are beyond our control. In those circumstances we must accept the fact that the river is flooding or we're under a tornado warning—then grab our most precious belongings and head for shelter.

On the other hand, there are plenty of other aspects to the different seasons that *are* within our control, which leads to the next principle.

6. The way we handle one season profoundly impacts how we experience the seasons that follow.

I grew up on the prairies, and it seemed to me the farmers were always complaining. We'd have a beautiful winter's day, and they would bemoan how the lack of snow would affect soil moisture in spring. A sunny summer would prompt them to pine for more rain. Then it would rain in autumn, and they'd worry about getting the harvest in before the advent of winter frosts.

These farmers were wise, of course, to pay close attention to the seasons because their livelihoods depended on successfully navigating all four of them. Bumper crops don't happen by accident; they're the cumulative result of careful effort over the preceding seasons.

So, too, the way we handle each season dramatically affects the ones that follow. Like the weather, life's circumstances aren't always optimal. Some of the winters we go through in life are harsher and colder than others, some of our summers are drier and hotter, and sometimes our springs and autumns are stormy. In our seasonal circumstances, just as in nature, we can't control the weather—but we can determine our responses to it. The choices we make today produce future results at compound interest. The biblical principle is relentlessly true, in a multitude of ways: "Whatever one sows, that will he also reap" (Galatians 6:7, ESV).

For example, the effort we make during our summers determines the rewards of autumn and the comfort of winter. Some people simply can't bring themselves to toil in summer. As soon as it arrives, they look for the nearest shady tree to sit under. The problem is, you won't enjoy a bumper crop in autumn if you waste your summer taking siestas.

The most common violations of this principle are when people either try to rush into a new season too soon or hold on to one after its time is past. *Season rushers* are people who dash forward—into a relationship, a job offer, a commitment to serve others in some capacity, or whatever—before they're prepared. So often they fail to fully explore possible options in light of their goals and values in life and their calling from God.

Because these people don't take time to explore the new world they're entering, they limit their possibilities and often miss out on the wonder of their life's journey. They also set themselves up for a midlife crisis, boredom in their career, divorce, and other calamities.

People have far more choices than they realize. Spring is the time to investigate those opportunities.

God designed the seasons for a reason, and in each one, important developments must occur. When you attempt to cut short a divinely sanctioned process, you inevitably run into problems; you'll enter the next stage of your life unprepared.

In contrast to season rushers are *season graspers*. These people stubbornly cling to their current situations. They are preschoolers terrified of going to kindergarten, teenagers unwilling to assume more responsibility and get a job or go to college, or mothers unwilling to loosen the apron strings. They can be aging executives who dread retirement like Superman hates kryptonite because they fear they'll lose their power and influence. Oftentimes our family, friends, and colleagues recognize when it's time for us to move on to the next season of our lives, even as we stubbornly refuse to acknowledge the obvious.

The problem is that we cannot get the most out of life if we hold on to a season past its expiration date. In trying to do so, we deprive ourselves of the freshness and wonder of the new season awaiting us.

The way to live the most fulfilling life possible is to squeeze every ounce of life out of each season in turn—to continually grow in purpose, passion, and perspective—and then to boldly move on to the next season when it comes.

Yet so many people, who may reside on the earth for seventy-five or ninety or a hundred years, will really *live* only a small fraction of that time. They squander their lives in innumerable ways and for all sorts of reasons. I've been inside maximum security prisons. I've walked down death row and talked with people who have made horrific mistakes and who were going to pay the ultimate penalty. Though they may have eventually gained a proper perspective on their lives, they had tragically slammed the door closed to most of life's possibilities.

Most of us will never travel down such a dismal road. But a sobering question intrigues me: Why do normal people, with ordinary opportunities and possibilities, choose to accept less than the best life available? To me, this phenomenon is bewildering. Life is too precious to waste even one minute, let alone years. Yet people do it by the millions all the time. What could be more tragic?

7. We can—and often do—fail to recognize and understand our particular season.

This principle should be apparent already from what we just discussed, but let's think more about it.

God's gift of life is something we're to take day by day from His hand. Jesus taught us to pray, "Give us *this day* our *daily* bread" (Matthew 6:11; see also Proverbs 30:8; Isaiah 33:2). We're reminded that the Lord's mercies and compassions "are new *every morning*" (Lamentations 3:22–23). With every dawn we can sing with David, "Blessed be the Lord, who daily loads us with benefits" (Psalm 68:19). By divine design we have daily obligations to help and encourage other believers in the life of faith: "Exhort one another *daily,* while it is called 'Today'" (Hebrews 3:13). *Day by day by day* is the fundamental rhythm for living our lives in the sight of God.

But as we've seen in Ecclesiastes 3, those days all fit into larger patterns that God uniquely designed for each of us—our seasonal rhythms. There's a right time, there's an appropriate season, for everything we do, and it's our responsibility to discern it. When we get that right—when we're in the center of God's timetable—the result is that life is "beautiful" (verse 11). Our existence is never more pleasing and harmonious than when we're busy with the right things at the correct moment. There's a meaningful wholeness that's deeply satisfying.

We have every reason to be "season sensitive" in how we live our lives, and yet so often we're blinded to this perspective. Why?

It's no secret, really. The same inherent sinfulness that blocks us from recognizing so many of God's truths, blessings, and principles is also at work to hinder our perception of the seasons God has designed into each of our lives.

As fallen creatures in a sin-filled world, we can't expect to be fully and automatically aware of all the seasonal transitions God is leading us into. We need His help to keep from either jumping ahead or falling behind.

Some of us are more cautious in nature, others more daring, but the fact is, on various occasions we're all tempted to get ahead of God, and we're all sluggish at times in moving forward with Him. When we finally recognize the extent of these tendencies of ours, then we're ready to receive the gracious assistance that God sends our way in abundance through His Word and by His Spirit.

When we admit, as Paul did, "I have the desire to do what is right, but not the ability to carry it out" (Romans 7:18, ESV), then we're primed for the kind of guidance God wants to give us at every stage and in every season.

But it doesn't happen automatically.

8. Understanding our seasons of life requires a vital, open, trusting relationship with God.

In the beautiful passage in Proverbs 8 where personified Wisdom speaks as a representative of God's discernment, counsel, and insight, Wisdom tells us, "Blessed is the man who listens to me, watching daily at my gates" (verse 34). By the habit of daily listening for God's wisdom in the Scriptures, made alive by the Holy Spirit, we're to stay sensitive to whatever changes in His timetable He brings our way. We heed His command: "Therefore do not be unwise, but understand what the will of the Lord is" (Ephesians 5:17).

We're wise and not unwise when we regularly pray, "Lord, what would You have me to do *now*?" Knowing that everything in our lives has an eternal purpose and an appropriate schedule, we don't thoughtlessly charge ahead in whatever we feel pressured to do, or whatever we're drawn naturally to undertake, or whatever others are telling us to do. That doesn't mean we abandon unfinished responsibilities; if God has led us to begin something, that's plenty of evidence that He wants us to complete it, with excellence and integrity. But we're constantly facing various new options, opportunities, invitations, and attractions. Only by listening to the Lord, "watching daily at His gates," can we gain heaven's perspective to recognize how these things fit (or don't fit) into the seasonal schedule God has us in at the moment.

That's something we'll never do unless we trust His wise sovereignty over everything He calls us to and over everything He brings our way, in His perfect timing. When we relax in that kind of trusting relationship with the Lord, we're able to hear and believe His promise: "I will instruct you and teach you in the way you should go; I will guide you with My eye" (Psalm 32:8).

9. We experience different seasons in different aspects of our lives.

Life might be simpler if everyone was in the exact same season or if every aspect of our lives was in the identical season. But God, in His infinite capacity to diversify His creation, did not make life that way. The reality is that we can be in one particular season in regard to the stage of our family's development yet be in a very different season in terms of our career. Meanwhile we can also be experiencing still other seasonal differences in our various relationships and friendships outside the home, in our ministry opportunities, and in whatever other important endeavors and pursuits take up our time, energy, and thoughts.

Related to all this is the obvious fact that people around us—even those closest to us—won't necessarily be in the same seasonal configuration that we are. As you might expect, a lot of friction can occur when two people in different seasons fail to perceive each other's point of view.

Imagine a man who's spent years laboring in the same job but then in his forties launches his own company. It's a new spring season in his life. Careerwise, everything is new and exhilarating for him. He's consumed with fresh opportunities and challenges and can talk of nothing else.

Meanwhile his wife is grieving. She spent her child-rearing years at home tending their children and did a marvelous job. But now their youngest is a high school senior and will soon leave for college. So much is drawing to a close for her. Sometimes she feels bewildered as questions surface about her future role, activities, and responsibilities. She has loved what she has done with her life thus far, but the future looks dark, nebulous, and purposeless. It's a winter season for her. While she's happy for her husband, she wishes he was more understanding of her natural grief as a wonderful season of her life comes to an aching end.

Or imagine a woman who has finally found the career of her dreams. She feels challenged and stretched as never before. She wants to talk with her parents about the new business she's involved in, but they've recently retired and are having the time of their lives golfing and traveling with friends. The rat race of the business world is behind them now, and they're reluctant to engage on more than a surface level with the business concerns and fears that their daughter expresses.

Or consider the "worship wars" that arise in many churches. The young adults in a church are typically experiencing springtime in a multitude of ways, and it's natural for them to test limits and to challenge old habits. What better place to experiment than with the music and other aspects of their Sunday experience at church? It's time for something different and fresh; out with the old and in with the new!

Meanwhile that church is also home to many senior adults who are entering a winter season. In several aspects of life, much of what was dear to them has already come to an end. In their complex and multilayered grief over this, they look to the church as the one sanctuary where their experience remains constant—where they're surrounded by familiar hymns, customs, and traditions, the things that always brightened their souls and cheered their hearts in the past. No wonder they're upset with any who seek to change this bastion of stability in their lives.

The interpersonal clash of seasons is not just a generational conflict. Anyone going through a time of spring may be open to change and new beginnings, regardless of their age. Likewise, people in winter, at whatever age, may be resistant to further alterations in their routines and habits.

Resisting or accepting change isn't merely about how many birthdays we've had; it also has a great deal to do with our understanding of life's seasons and the opportunities each one provides. I've met grandparents who found such joy in actively participating in their grandchildren's lives that they chose to attend the contemporary service at their church so they could worship with their grandchildren. To their surprise, they grew to enjoy the newer tunes and heavier beat.

One crucial key to successfully relating to others is recognizing the multiplicity of overlapping seasons in those around you. It's what makes our relationships so rich, yet it also can easily lead to conflict. We're wise not only to identify the seasonal situation we're personally experiencing but also to discern which season others are going through so that we know how best to relate to them. In light of this particular time frame, there are always healthy and unhealthy ways to interact with others.

Are you close to others who happen to be winding down certain aspects of their lives? One way to encourage them is to help them celebrate what they've already experienced and attained so they can look back on their experiences with satisfaction and gratitude, which in turn can yield greater freedom to let go.

Are others you know gearing up for a springtime of new endeavors? They'll often be encouraged by the kind of personal affirmations that serve to squelch any fears or uneasiness they might have in facing new requirements and unknown circumstances.

Suppose you go for coffee with a group of friends who are all in different seasons. What will you talk about?

One friend may be in winter, experiencing nostalgia for what's ending at this point in life as well as trepidation over what's next—creating an urgent need to hear the assuring words, "Your best days are not behind you." Another friend meanwhile is in spring. She has entered a new relationship and is full of excitement and questions about the future. Yet another is in a summer mode of long hours of labor and feeling overwhelmed and in need of a refreshing break. Another friend in autumn is riding high, having recently been recognized for her success and expertise after long years in her chosen career. She wants advice in determining where to invest her energies next.

Anyone who understands life's seasons is able to relate meaningfully to a wide variety of people. If you think everyone should view the world from the same vantage point as you do, you're in for some awkward conversations! If you're in winter, you may view people in spring as naive, immature, or out of touch with the real world. You may grow impatient with people in summer who seem to be consumed with their own responsibilities. It might be hard for you to be around people in autumn who are hitting their peak just as you're coming down from yours.

It's all a matter of perspective. The world would have far less conflict if people understood how to relate to others in light of seasonal differences.

10. We're meant to thrive in every season.

Jesus once explained that the reason He came to earth was so people could (1) have life and (2) experience it *abundantly* (John 10:10). I don't think it's news to you that there are countless people today who are *existing* but not truly *living.*

That's a tragedy, because we live our lives only once. Whether we're prepared or not for what's ahead, life is steadily progressing, minute by minute, day by day, year by year. I certainly don't intend to waste the remainder of my life wistfully reminiscing about the glory years of the past. I suspect God has some pretty amazing things still to come! I hope you feel the same way about your one, precious, nontransferable life. If not, I hope I can change your view by the time you've finished this book.

I'm convinced that God intends for us to thrive in *every* season of life. Some people instinctively know how to enjoy each of nature's seasons to the maximum extent. In spring they're out planting a garden or playing on a local softball team or practicing their golf swing. Summer comes, and they head off to the beach with their family, or perhaps they build a new deck. Autumn rolls around, and they go hiking or celebrate the harvest with friends and relatives. Winter doesn't slow them down either; they take ski trips or coach a basketball team. Whatever season they're in, they manage to receive the full benefit.

That is how God intends for people to experience the seasons of life—to the max.

Some seasons may be more difficult and some more personally or financially rewarding, but every season holds potential for personal enrichment. (We'll have more to say about this later.)

MAKING A DIFFERENCE

So what does it matter if you have a good awareness of the existence of these seasons?

Well, not much—*if* you fail to apply your awareness to the larger scope of God's calling in your life. You may as well ignore the truth of life's seasonal dimensions if you're fine with getting dragged down by seasonal changes you don't like...or if you're itching for a fight and want to actively resist these changes...or if you're determined to cling, no matter what, to the comfortable routines you've already established.

But both you and I desire something better than that—I'm sure of it. And seeing exactly why it's better is what we'll explore next.

REFLECT AND RESPOND

1. When you think about the best time in your life, do you look to your past, to the future, or to the present? What does your answer tell you?

2. Look back over the Ten Laws of the Seasons of Life (the numbered, bold-type statements throughout this chapter). Which of these ten were you least aware of before? Which of the ten do you think are most significant for you to fully understand? Are there any you disagree with?

3. Have you been tempted to hold on to a season too long or to rush to the next season too soon? If you have, what motivated you to do so? What were the consequences?

4. Are you currently wasting your life in some way? How might you be doing that? What should you do about it? Have you somehow settled for mediocrity rather than thriving?

5. Which season of life has generally impacted you the most?

4

Benefits of a Seasonal Perspective

What do we gain from being "season sensitive"?

Maybe the most important benefit is that a seasonal perspective on life promotes our dependence on God. As we observed in the last chapter, without God's constant help we can't properly identify and fully understand which season we're in and all that it requires from us. It's the kind of help we seek more readily when we're maintaining a seasonal outlook. Instead of the deadening effect of assuming we've already "arrived"—having reached a plateau where we can finally settle down—we'll hunger for God to keep showing us the new stages and phases and adventures He's planned for us. A seasonal perspective makes it easier to deepen our *passion* for all God calls us to in every stage of life.

As we live out our God-inspired, God-dependent adventure, there are four special benefits of a seasonal outlook that I want to emphasize for you.

Clearer Purpose

A seasonal perspective on life gives you a better grid for understanding your unfolding *purpose* in life—that thrilling sense of *knowing where you're going,* which in turn motivates you to adequately *prepare* for that particular journey and destination.

Recently I was scheduled to speak at a conference in Alabama. The morning I was to leave, I hurriedly threw some clothes into a suitcase. It was to be a brief trip, so I packed light. Upon my arrival there was no one to greet me.

Now, I travel a lot, and I encounter all kinds of well-meaning but sometimes absent-minded people who've been assigned to pick me up at the airport. I appreciate the sacrifice they make to help me, but my traveling experiences have provoked some compelling questions.

For instance, why does a person meet a traveler at the airport without making sure he knows what said traveler looks like? I can't tell you how many people have been obliviously waiting for me at an exit while I walked right past them. Clearly I don't look like what some people imagine!

And why do volunteers graciously offer to pick someone up at the airport but then have no room for luggage because their trunk is crammed with golf clubs and sundry objects belonging to their children?

Or why do would-be chauffeurs arrive late, leaving you waiting by an empty baggage carousel, wondering what to do? Later, explaining their delay, they'll mention how traffic is always bad at this time of day. (Which begs the question: If they knew that, why didn't they leave earlier for the airport?) Or what about people who ask you to call them after your flight arrives but they give you the wrong phone number? Then there are those who forget where they parked their car, so you have to walk around the parking garage helping them locate their vehicle.

On this particular day my befuddled new friend had committed most of the aforementioned errors. I was trying to be patient and preserve my Christian charity while my driver vainly attempted to cram my suitcase into the backseat of his overcrowded SUV. Trying to kill time while he rearranged his belongings in the backseat and pondering why people set out on a journey without first considering their destination, I bent down to tighten the shoelaces on my right shoe.

That's when I noticed.

On my right foot was an old black shoe I hadn't worn in years. "What on earth is *that* shoe doing on my foot?" I mused. I can honestly say that until that moment I had never dreaded looking at my left foot. Steeling myself for the worst, I inhaled deeply and glanced leftward. My worst fears were realized.

Sitting snugly on my left foot was my good black shoe, which, despite its many notable qualities, did not—in even the slightest detail—resemble the old black shoe encasing my right foot.

For the remainder of the trip as I stood before hundreds of people, my shoes were as dissimilar as Batman and Robin, men and women, cats and dogs… Well you get the idea. I was humiliated! (Of course, when you're a public speaker or author, there's really never a bad experience, merely a fresh illustration.)

I was guilty of the same basic error as so many of my airport companions: I hadn't carefully considered where I was going and thus hadn't properly prepared for the journey. I'd just shown up. And when you "just show up" in life, the results are seldom to your liking.

In a memorable encounter in Wonderland between Alice and the Cheshire Cat, Alice asks:

> "Would you tell me, please, which way I ought to walk from here?"
>
> "That depends a good deal on where you want to get to," said the Cat.
>
> "I don't much care where—" said Alice.
>
> "Then it doesn't matter which way you walk," said the Cat.[8]

If you don't know where your life is going, any route will get you there. One job that pays the bills will appear as good as another (even better, if the remuneration is higher). One spouse or church or house or career will seem as acceptable as another if you have no sense of where your life is headed and what help you need to arrive at your destination. But when your life is guided by a sense of purpose and direction, you recognize how profoundly every decision you make either draws you closer to or moves you away from where your life is meant to be.

When the Old Testament prophet Jeremiah was still a teenager, God assured him, "Before I formed you in the womb I knew you; before you were born I sanctified you; I ordained you a prophet to the nations" (Jeremiah 1:5). David affirms in Psalm 139 that even before we were born, God had a purpose for our lives (verse 16).

In the brief period in which we inhabit the globe, it's our sacred obligation to determine why our Creator granted us the gift of life and placed us on the planet at this specific time and place. "Be ashamed to die," educator and statesman Horace Mann once declared, "until you win some victory for humanity."

Too many people are merely putting in time on earth before exiting stage left, thereby tragically missing out on the fulfillment that life can offer. In 2002 Rick Warren wrote *The Purpose Driven Life*, and its amazing popularity provided clear evidence that people desperately want to know their life's purpose. Are our lives merely accidents of fate? Do we simply try to get by, doing the best we can before, as Hamlet eloquently stated, we've "shuffled off this mortal coil"?

It's relatively easy to identify people who are living intentional lives. They're usually focused, and they dislike squandering their time (or their lives). Their primary goal isn't to get by until they retire; rather, they enjoy their work and their lives.

A few years ago *USA Today* conducted an online poll asking people whether they would continue going to work if they won the lottery. As you might expect, 67 percent of the people claimed they probably would not. Only 11 percent of the respondents believed they would definitely remain at their job even if they no longer needed the money. While some people can't imagine working a solitary day if they don't have to, others get up every morning to fulfill their life's purpose rather than merely to earn a paycheck.

It's easy to waste time. We all do it occasionally. Some people, however, manage to fritter away most of their lives. They allow themselves to remain stuck in a job they hate. Or they're careless in relationships and find themselves continually enmeshed in conflict and frustration. They may be simply bored with their lives. Many have never considered what their life's purpose is, so they lack passion for anything they do.

Without a sense of purpose, life loses its direction. But a seasonal perspective serves us by continually bringing our purpose and direction back into focus.

FREEDOM TO LIVE IN THE PRESENT

My wife, Lisa, has an older sister named Connie. She was pretty zany in college while the two sisters were roommates. One day Connie noticed Lisa had a bright red apple on her desk for an afternoon snack.

"Oh! I love apples!" Connie exclaimed. "Can I have one bite?"

Thinking it couldn't hurt to concede one chomp to her older sis, Lisa consented. With that, Connie immediately dug her fangs deeply into the fruit, and then, without ever removing her teeth from the apple, she systematically turned it around in her mouth until she had bared it to its core.

"Tanku," Connie blurted through swollen cheeks—and off she went.

While Connie might be challenged on her roommate etiquette, no one could doubt her enthusiasm for apples!

That kind of zealous attitude is the way God intends for us to embrace life. God didn't design our lives to be fussily picked at and complained about. He intends for life to be *savored*. God meant it when he declared that life was "very good" (Genesis 1:31). Of course, Adam and Eve got to hang out in a perfect garden—long before pollution, terrorists, and people driving under the speed limit in the passing lane. Nonetheless, considering we came from dust and we're returning to the same, God was declaring that our brief earthly sojourn is a privilege as well as a breathtaking opportunity.

In fact, when you consider the miracle that took place for you to be conceived, then to survive pregnancy, childbirth, childhood diseases, and innumerable potential tragedies, your life today is a bona fide miracle.

Are you treating each new day as a divine gift?

In the last chapter we looked briefly at season rushers and season graspers. We must be constantly alert to those all-too-common tendencies. Have you fully considered how you might be limiting yourself by falling into one of those traps?

Some people really don't like the stage of life they currently occupy. They're impatient to get somewhere else.

I remember my son Mike as a young boy being consumed with the interminable wait for Christmas and the anticipated windfall. In exasperation he declared, "I just wish I could fast-forward my life!"

That's a widespread feeling. The four-year-old constantly asks her mother when she can go to school, while the teenager or college student desperately wants to be done with it. The middle-aged professional continually dreams of retirement. Parents count the years (or hours, depending on the child) until they have an empty nest. These individuals are dissatisfied with their present circumstances and assume their lives will automatically improve at a future point in time. The problem is that they waste amazing life potential in their present episode while waiting for the next act to begin.

Jonathan Swift sagely advised, "May you live all the days of your life." Too often we truly *live* only at brief intervals.

A good friend once asked me how my wife and I were doing. I replied that we were "okay" but if we could just "get through" a particularly busy time, I believed things would be much better. My friend, knowing me well, suggested that we don't "get through" life in the same manner we endure a root canal. We *enjoy* life.

The reality is that we pass through life only once. Let's say you're fifteen. Eventually you may live to be ninety-nine, but you'll be a fifteen-year-old for only one brief year! It represents a mere fraction of your lifespan. So why be anxious to turn sixteen—or to be eighteen or twenty or thirty? Those years will come soon enough!

Likewise, why get anxious to be old enough to go to college, enter the work force, start a family, have grandchildren, or retire? Too many people squander major portions of their lives because they're continually gazing at life's distant shores instead of opening their eyes to amazing opportunities lying before them today.

Why is it that we often don't appreciate what we have until it's gone?

Meanwhile an equal number of dissatisfied people are desperately trying not to fast-forward their days but to rewind them. They're convinced their best days are over. The middle-aged man tries to stuff his overfed torso into his high school football jacket to relive the glory days. The mother of three grows weary of child rearing and dreams of her carefree college years. The senior adult wistfully recalls his prime, when he was a mover and shaker in the business world. Such people bore their friends retelling their threadbare war stories and reminiscing about their Camelot days.

While it's natural to fondly recall times when we had more energy, influence, and excitement or less body mass, we can never go back to that time (or perhaps to that waist size).

Besides, our current stage of life is seldom as bad as we might think.

I remember going on a ski outing with my family and some of our relatives. During a lull in the conversation, my brother-in-law Gerry broke the silence by stating, "I just realized I'm going to turn fifty this year. I have to start thinking about things."

"Like what?" one of the kids asked.

"Well…like *death!*" he replied. In a flash, family members began excusing themselves and hurriedly hitting the slopes.

Well, it's true that the moment of our last dying breath is an approaching reality, and we're foolish to ignore it. But shouldn't the thought of it lead constructively to a fresh commitment to living vitally in the here and now?

The fact is, every stage of life has aspects to be cherished. There's no point in compulsively wasting time either by peering into the future or by nostalgically recalling the past. (After all, nostalgia isn't what it used to be!)

Ultimately, we can only live *today*—in the particular season God has us in at the moment. Keeping a seasonal outlook reminds us of the uniqueness of the particular days unfolding before us.

FREEDOM FROM BITTERNESS AND REGRETS

I once had a dull professor who annoyed me. He devoted most of his class time ranting about what he disliked while neglecting to cover the material that would later show up on our midterm exam. But one thing he said stuck with me. He related how, when he was requested to preach in churches (the thought of anyone *willingly* inviting him to stand behind a lectern baffled me), he would examine the pastor's library and determine what year the minister had "died."

This odd observation may well have been further evidence of my professor's cynicism and arrogance, but since then, on my own numerous visits to pastoral and executive offices, I've often been struck by the sparseness of their reading materials.

That professor's comment intrigues me. Can you "die" before you draw your last breath?

Perhaps you've undergone a divorce. As painful as that is, especially if your spouse betrayed you, it shouldn't be a death sentence. But it becomes one for those who remain bitter for the remainder of their lives. I know one woman who never recovered from the betrayal she felt when her husband of twenty-five years filed for divorce. Years later, regardless of whether people were discussing the weather or who would win the World

Series, she would invariably bring every conversation around to how terribly her former husband had treated her. Her divorce brought her life to an abrupt halt; now she merely puts in time waiting for her physical death to catch up to the emotional demise she experienced years earlier.

A great many individuals have suffered some form of significant loss at least once in their lives. Parents may tragically lose a child to an accident or disease. Longtime loyal employees may be unfairly dismissed. People experience heart-wrenching broken relationships and become estranged from family or friends. A traumatic loss (or multiple losses) can inflict a death sentence on people's joy and contentment if the remainder of their existence is wasted in bitterness and resentment.

Conversely, others who've endured unimaginable anguish have nevertheless refused to allow their suffering to define them. Some of these people were horribly abused and neglected as children. Others received physical injuries that left them permanently impaired. Some were treated in the most disrespectful and callous fashion at their jobs. Yet they chose not to while away their lives consumed by bitterness. Instead, they realized that although they had suffered deeply, time had not stopped. The clock was still ticking, and they wanted to make the most of their remaining days.

I know a woman who watched her husband and two sons grow deaf from a genetic disease. Rather than become bitter, she learned sign language so she could sign during the services at her church. Today this woman is thrilled to see deaf people from her community attending her church. I know several people who suffered sexual abuse as children. Today they volunteer to help and encourage others who have likewise suffered. These are people who have chosen to live life to the full. They grasped at joy even as heartache had earlier clasped its tenacious jaws onto them.

There are many degrees of regret in life. I'm not referring to the kind that results from hurriedly choosing Mexican food at the airport before embarking on a four-hour cross-country flight (although such decisions cry out for sober second thought). I'm talking here about regrets that cling to our souls and can haunt us for decades.

Most people have regrets of some kind; no one has an unblemished past. But our remorse over bygone days must not be allowed to hijack our lives. We can't go back and change what we did previously. We can learn from our mistakes and enthusiastically live today.

That's why the apostle Paul, who had been complicit in the murder of Stephen, forged his way forward by "forgetting those things which are behind" (Philippians 3:13). Paul certainly must have agonized over his role in the murder of a righteous man. But there was nothing he could do to change his former actions or their outcome. All he could do was live his life well in the present.

Some regrets stem from major mistakes we made in life. Others result from odd experiences. I experienced such an event when I was a senior in high school. My algebra teacher had taken a liking to me. I'm not sure why; I was anything but a stellar student. But after every lecture, while the other students completed their homework in class, he would stop by my desk and banter with me.

One day while teaching, he suffered a severe leg cramp and fell to the floor in excruciating pain. Every eye in the classroom turned to me. They all knew I was his favorite student. My friends quietly urged me to "do something." Yet I was frozen. I felt extremely self-conscious about rushing to the front of the classroom and pulling on my teacher's leg! So I sat glued to my desk.

Finally another student arose from his desk and helped our fallen professor. I felt terrible. Worse yet, my relationship with that teacher was irreparably damaged. He stopped talking with me after class. And though I may be imagining a connection with that incident, my grade plummeted from a solid B to a shaky D.

What bothered me more than my lost relationship—and my realization that I would never qualify for engineering school—was my failure of nerve. I had allowed fear to prevent me from taking action. For months, even years, afterward, I was still trying to figure out why I'd failed to help someone in need that day. Was I a coward? Was I an unreliable friend? Was I driven by others' opinions?

Ultimately I concluded two things as a result of that incident.

First, no matter how many times I replayed the event in my mind, it would always end the same way. I couldn't change the past, regardless of how ashamed I was of it.

Second, I resolved that if I saw someone in need in the future, I wouldn't allow myself to freeze up in fear. I would force myself out of my chair and take action. I don't want to have additional regrets in the future.

Since then I've faced some extremely difficult and unpleasant tasks, but I've generally willed myself into action even when my natural inclination was to hold back and hope someone else would come to the rescue. To allow a previous failure to predetermine and limit the remainder of my life would be a terrible waste.

When we recognize that life cycles through seasons of preparation and molding (painful at times) and on to seasons of fulfillment and usefulness, we can find ourselves liberated from regret and shame as we keep moving forward.

Escape from Mediocrity

Some people squander their lives by settling for mediocrity—simply getting by from day to day. Modern society is obsessed with living *long* but not necessarily with living *well*. The key to a good life is not the number of years listed in your obituary but how you spent the time you had.

I had the privilege of meeting a sweet young teen named Hannah Sullivan. At age sixteen she attended a Christian retreat for teenagers at her church. The speaker told them that it's often during the storms of life that God works most powerfully in and through us. Hearing that, Hannah prayed for a storm in her young life so people could see Jesus in her. She couldn't have known then that a storm was already looming.

Very soon afterward, Hannah was diagnosed with grade 4 glioblastoma multiforme—a brain tumor. She endured surgery as well as chemotherapy and radiation. Initial results looked promising. But soon the cancer returned. On February 26, 2009, Hannah died. She was only seventeen.

Throughout her ordeal, Hannah did what she had prayed. She displayed a tenacious faith in God, regardless of her circumstances. I had the privilege of being with Hannah in her church and watching her boldly encourage her church family to trust in the Lord.

Sharing in Hannah's suffering and seeing her example, her parents and sister grew in their own faith. Ultimately they, along with a couple who had lost their son during the war in Afghanistan, established While We're Waiting (www.whilewerewaiting.org) to lovingly minister to families who have lost a child and are waiting until heaven to be reunited.

"We have peace that she's in heaven," Hannah's father says. "She is where she was created to be. What more could we want for our child?… The fact that Hannah prayed for a storm to give God glory—we don't feel like we need to waste that storm."

Hannah didn't live long, but she lived well. And her legacy continues.[9]

Some people settle for a life that's far below their capacity. They stop dreaming, stop trying, stop growing. They may live to be a hundred, but they settle for existing—just getting by. We ought never to settle for less than the best life we're capable of living.

I was intrigued by the story of Peter Arnell. He led a successful Manhattan marketing firm, promoting such companies as Samsung, Chanel, Fendi, Pepsi, Home Depot, Reebok, and Mars. Yet while he always marketed his products in the best light possible, he was careless with his own life. He eventually allowed his weight to balloon to more than 400 pounds.

One day he realized that by maintaining his current lifestyle, he wouldn't be around to enjoy his grandchildren. So Arnell rebranded himself, made drastic life changes, and lost 256 pounds in the process.[10] Here was a man who grew tired of the excuses and bad habits of a lifetime, so he radically recast himself into the kind of person who could thrive.

It has been my privilege to know many people who decided life was too brief and valuable to waste by wallowing in mediocrity or excuses, so they made changes. One young woman I know lacked the confidence to go to university right after high school, so she took a job as a waitress. A year stretched into two, then three. At age thirty, she was in management and making good money. Yet when she took stock of her life, she realized she was nowhere closer to achieving her dream of becoming a school-teacher. She could summon a thousand excuses for not attending university, but she couldn't assuage her deep desire to experience a life she could be proud of. She took out a student loan, enrolled in university, and today is an outstanding elementary school teacher.

Another woman, Diane, longed to travel abroad. She'd never done so because her husband, while perhaps not a skinflint, did not suffer from wanderlust. He hated air travel and enjoyed remaining close to home. Worse, however, was his refusal to let her participate in any of their church's international missions trips.

When he passed away, the first thing Diane did with her husband's insurance money was to sign up for her church's next trip to Southeast Asia. She was eighty-two at the time. She bubbled with exuberance; the people on her team said she was over-the-top excited the entire trip. She served enthusiastically each day and inspired everyone she worked with.

While I was at her church, I noticed a sign-up list in the foyer for next summer's mission trip—and Diane's name was hurriedly scribbled at the top of the page! This dear octogenarian couldn't change her past, but she could live zealously in her new season.

Living life to the full doesn't require taking luxury Caribbean cruises every winter or buying new sets of designer clothing each spring (although my daughter is game if I'm paying). It means you squeeze everything out of life that God makes available to you at the time. Often the most mean-ingful moments don't cost a lot or make headlines, but they make life enjoyable.

I remember being an impoverished graduate student and taking my two preschool sons to a nearby lake to toss breadcrumbs to some none-too-shy ducks. My boys laughed uproariously!

And I recall one summer when Lisa and I were too broke to go on a vacation, so we borrowed my brother-in-law's modest pickup camper and parked it at a nearby campsite. I'll never forget the laughter pealing through the air on those summer evenings as our kids heard our stories about the goofy things their mom and dad had done in their youth. *That* was living! It wasn't going to be written up in the AAA travel magazine, but for us, in that season of our lives, we were living life to the max. Liv-ing well is not synonymous with living extravagantly.

And living well is something we're enabled increasingly to do as we recognize and appreciate the dynamic seasonal canopy that's spread over our lives like the ever-changing sky.

We're now almost ready to take a close look at each of the four recur-ring seasons in our lives—to explore what they really mean and what to expect with each one as we push forward in vibrant aliveness. All we need is some brief help in sharpening our skills of perception and applica-tion—and that's coming up next.

REFLECT AND RESPOND

1. As you reflect on the major points made in this chapter, what do you see—for yourself personally—as the most sig-nificant benefits of having a seasonal perspective on life?

2. Have you had some difficult seasons in the past? How have they affected your life since?

3. What's one thing you could do immediately that would make your life better? What has been stopping you from doing this?

4. Do you tend to live your life with gusto? Why or why not? Do you enjoy your current job or role in life? Why or why not?

5. Is your current life being hampered by regrets from the past? If so, what is one regret you have? What do you think God wants you to do about it? What is one thing you might do today that could prevent a regret in the future?

5

STRENGTHENING YOUR SEASONAL PERSPECTIVE

Let's reflect once more on the pattern from nature that portrays the seasonal flow in our lives.

Think of it this way: God created the universe. He fashioned the relatively tiny Milky Way galaxy along with countless others. Every galaxy, star, and planet was designed to follow certain universal rules. Then, here on planet Earth, God established an amazing environment governed by the perpetual ebb and flow of seasons. All around us is a system controlled by predictable, repeatable, and unchanging patterns.

At the pinnacle of His creative work, God made people to dwell in and enjoy this fascinating environment. And in doing so, He didn't fashion beings who would follow different natural laws from those that govern the physical environment. (Try breaking the law of gravity, and you'll see what I mean.) God created humans to fit perfectly into the physical system He'd already designed. People are the apex of creation, but they're still a part of that creation.

So what does this mean for us?

Well, just as farmers must take the four seasons into account each year if they're to be successful, we must comprehend the ebb and flow of the seasons in our lives if we're going to thrive in each one. At times our lives may seem to be full of exciting new possibilities, while other periods may feel like all work and no play. We'll occasionally grow restless and sense that a change is coming, even before it actually occurs. And we'll find that activities or relationships we have greatly enjoyed and depended on in the past are drawing to a close.

As we encounter such experiences, do we understand why these particular things are happening at this specific time? Will we recognize each seasonal change and respond in a way that's in harmony with what's occurring?

That's what we'll seek to examine together in the rest of this book.

As we launch into a concentrated look at each of the four seasons we cycle through in all our earthly endeavors, I want to help you maximize the benefit you'll derive from each one. There are four major areas of your life that are affected every time you enter a new season. You'll see how these play out in the following chapters, but let me identify them for you here.

Your Identity

We each have a fundamental personality that we maintain throughout our lives. But I would suggest that every season of life adds new color and texture to the question *Who am I?*

There are those who emphasize that we are, after all, human *beings,* not human *doings.* While that's true, I believe that we come to truly know ourselves only through the course of what we do—our activities and relationships.

For example, does a monk living alone in a cave in Tibet really know himself? Suppose that after ten years of meditation the recluse finally achieves this self-realization: *I am a patient person.*

Great! He's so excited at this decade-long discovery that he travels to the nearest airport and boards a plane for the United States to share his insight with his spiritual guru. However, on board the jumbo jet he's seated next to an unruly two-year-old. Throughout the fifteen-hour transcontinental flight, the child shrieks at ear-piercing decibels and continually throws sticky, soggy Cheerios at the monk. The two-year-old's overwhelmed mother issues anemic threats of dire punishment but never actually follows through.

Fifteen hours after takeoff, when the plane finally lands, the exhausted hermit has gained a fresh revelation: *I am not a patient person.* His earlier theory about himself has been severely challenged by his experience! So he boards the next flight home to the tranquillity of his Tibetan cave, where he can strive once more to gain a better understanding of himself.

It's by reflectively living our lives before God and with others that we come to truly understand ourselves. Throughout our lives we'll be pondering questions about ourselves: Am I a self-focused teenager? a self-sacrificing parent? a good friend? a take-charge CEO? a doting grandparent? Each new season of life will shed fresh light and perspective on who we truly are.

YOUR RELATIONSHIPS

Throughout our lives we must learn to relate to and communicate with other people. As our identity matures, so should our relationships.

There's a world of difference between determining who your best friend is in elementary school and relating to your grandchildren. Each season brings a new constellation of relationships that, if navigated well, allows us to experience great satisfaction and joy.

Relationships aren't meant to remain static. As we enter each new season in life, we'll need different things from others, and their requirements of us will change as well. Relationships that don't change with the seasons are vulnerable to stagnation, conflict, and grief.

YOUR ROLES

Our roles in life often change with each new season.

In spring, we're often called to be learners and explorers. Whether we're negotiating our way around kindergarten, high school, or retirement, spring is when we explore new opportunities and discover how God designed us to thrive.

Summer calls for us to embrace our tasks, roll up our sleeves, and get to work. Our summer roles may be as diligent students, hardworking employees, tireless parents, or faithful volunteers.

In autumn we reach the peak of our labors. This is when we may be called upon to provide leadership or mentoring. It's the season when we should do more than perform our own work well; we should also encourage others in their endeavors.

Finally, winter is when we bring certain roles to an end. Perhaps you're a terrific basketball player in high school, but now you're in your senior year. Your coach asks you to focus on mentoring the freshmen and juniors on the team as they prepare to take your place. Our roles change as we enter each new season. The way we handle them largely determines whether we thrive or merely survive.

YOUR FAITH

Throughout life there are two persons you need to continually learn more about. The first is yourself (your identity); the other is God (your faith). It will take a lifetime to fully understand yourself and an eternity even to begin to comprehend God! How does a finite creature of dust, who lives in the temporal, physical world, come to any understanding of an infinite God who's eternal and invisible and who dwells in the supernatural realm? It takes time—an eternity of time!

A highly successful businessman named Job was considered the godliest person of his age, but after entering a particularly difficult season in his life, he concluded: "I have heard of You by the hearing of the ear, but now my eye sees You" (Job 42:5).

As the wanderer Jacob began a new season of his life living apart from his family and homeland, he had such a profound vision of God that he exclaimed: "Surely the LORD is in this place, and I did not know it" (Genesis 28:16).

Peter and his fishing buddies were experts on wind, weather, and waves. But one night they were caught in their boat during a violent storm in the middle of the sea. With one command, their leader, Jesus, calmed the tempest. Peter and his companions were so amazed that they queried, "Who can this be? For He commands even the winds and water, and they obey Him!" (Luke 8:25).

The apostle Paul declared that the driving aim of his life was to fully know Christ (Philippians 3:8–10). Perhaps no one in that day knew Christ better than Paul did, yet he recognized it would require the remainder of his life to obtain a full understanding of who Christ was.

In the evolving seasons of their lives, all these people were learning more about God. Likewise for us, each new season provides opportunities to know and experience God more fully and richly than we have before. What an amazing privilege!

THE RIGHT SPEED FORWARD

Each new season will introduce us to deeper levels of understanding of our identity, our relationships, our roles, and our faith. It's up to us to receive what God offers us in each one.

Whether you're in your twenties, forties, or eighties, my goal in this book is to help you embrace your present season with enthusiasm and eager anticipation. Don't be in such a hurry to move on that you miss the incredible things God has placed along the way.

As one of my sons remarked when his brother tried to inhale a deluxe, fully loaded burger in three bites, "Dude! Slow down and enjoy the journey!" Good advice for all of us.

So let's wrap our minds around what each season is really all about, season by season and chapter by chapter. Use what we'll discuss to reflect on *where you've been, where you are now,* and *where you're sure to be in the future.*

Meanwhile make your commitment now to make the most of every minute, come what may.

REFLECT AND RESPOND

1. Based on what you've read so far, what season best represents where you are right now in the most significant areas of your life? Remember, *spring* is about beginnings, *summer* is about the hard work that comes after you begin something, *autumn* is the harvest of your labors, and *winter* is when things wind down for that particular stage of life.

2. Take a moment and jot down a summary of the most significant current factors that you recognize in your identity, your roles, your relationships, and your faith. Then reflect on at least one insight into each of these four areas that you have learned during your current stage of life.

3. As you grow in having a stronger, clearer seasonal perspective on your life, what kinds of changes do you think this is most likely to bring about for you?

PART TWO

EMBRACING
EACH SEASON

6

Spring: The Time of Beginnings

Springtime brims with beginnings, and those beginnings are often generated by dreams.

When my son Mike was a preschooler, he played for hours with the children in our student housing complex in Texas (where I was a graduate student). Their favorite game was the politically incorrect cowboys and Indians. Fierce battles were waged with no quarter given. Every little boy in the neighborhood intended to be a cowboy when he grew up.

Then we moved to Canada, where Mike started kindergarten. Sadly, school has a cruel way of crushing children's dreams. One afternoon Mike came home crestfallen. He'd been talking with other boys about their future plans for life after kindergarten. He was shocked to learn that not one of his classmates intended to become a cowboy.

Thoroughly disenchanted by this tragic discovery, he bared his thoughts to his mother: "Mom, none of my friends wants to be a cowboy… I'm gonna be all alone… Those Indians are going to *kill* me!"

He promptly adjusted his career aspirations and decided to become a policeman. (Having seen those men in blue, Mike knew he would have backup.)

Life is driven by dreams—so much so that when we stop dreaming, we start dying. Without a vision for our lives, we have no purpose or direction. That's why we need the returning flow of new springtimes in our lives, revitalizing our forward progress with fresh vision and understanding. Our springs bring forth new dreams of what God has in store for us.

THE PICTURE FOR US IN NATURE

This newness is wonderfully mirrored in nature, where spring can be magical. Its freshness and energy awaken the human spirit. After winter's icy tentacles release the earth from their frigid grasp, nature explodes in all its exuberant glory. The sun rises earlier and sets later. The mornings and evenings remain crisp, but the sun's rays now disperse the chill from the air during the course of the day. Warm breezes blow with renewed vigor, energizing trees and plants that have lain submissively dormant.

Winter's dull browns and grays are transformed into a dazzling bouquet of vivid colors and textures. Trees formerly stripped bare by chilly autumn winds now erupt with blossoms of vibrant red, pink, yellow, and white. Tiny green sprouts poke through the earth and eagerly stretch heavenward. The air is perfumed with a rich potpourri of aromas from flowers and plants emitting pollen and regaining their former vitality.

The sound of chirping reaches a frenzied pitch as birds search through winter's debris for daily nourishment. Geese return from their southern sojourns, honking each other onward across the bright sky. Newborn animals of every species take their tentative first steps as they enter the swelling animal kingdom and join in its frenetic pursuit of food. Creeks and rivers energetically roar with majestic strength as the spring runoff swells their banks. Spring possesses an energy that's unlike any other season.

Yet even as spring enthusiastically returns, winter's residue remains:

decaying leaves, dried flowers, broken branches, and even the carcasses of dead creatures. The previous generation becomes the seedbed for the next.

Of course, spring also has its dark side. In many areas spring is tornado season. Massive, dark, and deadly funnel clouds can descend upon a house or farm with devastating fury, hurling buildings and vehicles through the air like children's toys. Spring is also the most common season for floods. Runoff from melting snow can gorge streams and rivers until they ferociously rip away their banks and swallow up roads and buildings with cruel disdain.

Even as temperatures slowly ascend, spring snowfalls can bring a vengeful resurgence of winter. Living on the Canadian prairies for many years, I experienced the elation every year when winter seemed to finally draw to a close. But so often a late snowfall would strike in April (or May or June). If you've never experienced a springtime snowstorm, I assure you that pulling out a shovel in June to clear your driveway is demoralizing! Where I lived we learned not to set out flowering annuals before June 15, or the tender plants could be devastated by a late frost. Sometimes spring would briefly visit three or four times before finally deciding to stay.

Regardless of how harsh or tenacious winter may be, spring invariably emerges with stubborn determination to restore color to nature after months of white, gray, and brown. It's too early to predict the size of the eventual harvest, but the possibilities for the future are manifold and can appear limitless. It's difficult to be pessimistic when embracing the glory of spring that teems with promise.

What we see in nature's springtime is a picture of what we also find and experience when God brings times of new beginnings into our lives. These are the turning points that usher us into another stage, dimension, or opportunity. God brings them to us again and again. Whether we're five years old or ninety, there can always be another springtime appearing like magic in our lives.

THE PICTURE FOR US IN SCRIPTURE

From God's perspective we see this season reflected biblically in a continuing emphasis on newness and renewal. These are passages that often pulsate with their greatest impact upon us in the springtimes of our lives.

In the Bible we see the emphasis on springtime most powerfully in the resurrection of Jesus Christ and all the promise it holds for us. His resurrection means that "we also should walk in *newness of life*" (Romans 6:4). In our union with the risen Christ, our capacity for newness is endless because all believers "have put on *the new self,* which is being *renewed* in knowledge after the image of its creator" (Colossians 3:10, ESV). Every child of God is truly *"a new creation"* for whom "old things have passed away" and "all things have become *new*" (2 Corinthians 5:17). Toward God and toward each other, we now have full freedom to "serve in the *newness* of the Spirit" (Romans 7:6).

When Paul exhorts us to "be transformed by the *renewing* of your mind" (Romans 12:2), it's a calling that rings with special vitality in the springtimes that God graciously brings our way. Our spring seasons from God always offer us new opportunities to serve Him and bless others.

A New Earth and More

Again and again in the Scriptures we see men and women entering seasons of adventure marked by springtime surprises, freshness, and innovation. Appropriately, we can see this particularly in Genesis, the great book of beginnings.

Think of Noah emerging from the ark in that most dramatic of nature's springtimes (Genesis 8–9), when the earth put forth its green after the cataclysmic destruction of the flood. With the first-ever rainbow shining in the sky, with animals eagerly going forth to be fruitful and multiply and fill the earth, and with the Lord's fresh promises of His provision and protection resounding in people's hearts, this biblical moment mirrors the same kind of thrill that God extends to us in all our new beginnings.

It was in this moment that Noah did something simple yet profound that can be a message for us: "Noah began to be a farmer, and he planted a vineyard" (9:20). That's very much a depiction of what spring brings our way—a new identity with new responsibilities, new tasks, and new endeavors.

A Sojourn and Surprises

Next in Genesis we notice the various springtimes encountered in Abraham's life. We hear God telling him, "Go forth from your country, and from your relatives and from your father's house, to the land which I will show you" (12:1, NASB). The fresh opportunities we're afforded in our springtimes often require a turning away from the comfortable and the familiar, just as Abraham experienced in this moment.

This springtime redirection for Abraham was accompanied by an amazing promise from God: "I will make you a great nation; I will bless you and make your name great; and you shall be a blessing" (verse 2). Likewise for us, each time we follow God into our next springtime, we're accompanied by the divine promises necessary to experience meaning and success in the new leg of our journey.

And it can happen at any age. At this particular springtime moment for Abraham, he was already seventy-five (verse 4)!

As Abraham reached the new homeland God led him to, he marked the occasion by building altars to God (verses 7–8)—a reminder also for us to be proactive in gratitude and worship to the Lord as we enter each new stage of life.

After many years passed, Abraham encountered an even more profound springtime. Everything about it—his advanced age and especially

God's greater promise and calling—was more dramatic and intense than before:

> When Abram was ninety-nine years old, the LORD appeared to
> Abram and said to him, "I am Almighty God; walk before Me
> and be blameless. And I will make My covenant between Me
> and you, and will multiply you exceedingly." (17:1–2)

God now gave Abram the new name Abraham, meaning "father of a multitude." And the Lord greatly deepened His promise to him:

> I have made you a father of many nations. I will make you
> exceedingly fruitful; and I will make nations of you, and kings
> shall come from you. And I will establish My covenant between
> Me and you and your descendants after you in their generations,
> for an everlasting covenant, to be God to you and your descen-
> dants after you. (17:5–7)

Over the years, as we walk with God, we too will often see intensifi-cation in the springtimes we experience and what they mean for us. We'll see each one building upon what has happened before, and we'll sense God's holy purpose for our lives with greater clarity as well as increased complexity.

As a further shock for Abraham and his wife, Sarah, this particular new spring would usher them into parenthood—for Sarah at age ninety and her husband a decade older than that! As God said at the time, "Is anything too hard for the LORD?" (18:14). Obviously not. Again there are lessons here for us—one of them being that we're never to think of ourselves as too old for a dramatic new springtime of opportunity and promise from the Lord.

Abraham and Sarah's child—a son, Isaac—did indeed burst into their world according to God's perfect timetable, and afterward the newborn's mother would exclaim, "God has made me laugh, and all who hear will laugh with me" (21:6). A worthy example, I'd say, of the right approach to launching into any God-given spring!

Love Story

Multiple springtimes for others continue to unfold before us in the pages of Genesis, each one offering further perspective and instruction regarding our own springtimes.

In the generation that followed Abraham, we see a new spring unfold for a young woman named Rebekah. Imagine her surprise when a traveler showed up at her family's residence to announce a long-distance marriage proposal from the traveler's master, a distant relative of hers. That relative, of course, was Abraham, and the proposal involved Isaac, now grown to a young man.

Rebekah's father and older brother heard this surprising proposal and discerned the hand of God in it. So they sought Rebekah's response to the matter: "They called Rebekah and said to her, 'Will you go with this man?'" Rebekah's simple answer—"I will go" (24:58)—is itself a concise picture of brave commitment in the face of the unknown, a valuable asset in all our springtimes.

The narrative of Isaac and Rebekah is a true love story, and we go on to read how Isaac "took Rebekah and she became his wife, and he loved her" (verse 67). But love doesn't ward off life's tribulations, and this couple's next spring would be slow in coming. Rebekah was barren. Isaac, her loving husband, responded well to this crisis: "Now Isaac pleaded with the LORD for his wife, because she was barren; and the LORD granted his plea, and Rebekah his wife conceived" (25:21). Here's a good reminder that the springtimes we often yearn for most may not surface unless we seek the Lord and faithfully pray for them.

Then came another crisis for this young family: "There was a famine in the land" (26:1). Isaac resolved to take his family to Egypt as refugees. But God intervened—and in the process He brought Isaac into the experience of a sweeter, more profound springtime, in line with the divine encounters his father Abraham had experienced:

> The LORD appeared to him and said: "*Do not go down to Egypt;* live in the land of which I shall tell you. Dwell in this land, and *I will be with you and bless you;* for to you and your descendants I give all these lands, and I will perform the oath which I swore to Abraham your father. And I will make your descendants multiply as the stars of heaven; I will give to your descendants all these lands; and in your seed all the nations of the earth shall be blessed." (verses 2–4)

Isaac obeyed, and God again proved Himself faithful:

> And Isaac sowed in that land and reaped in the same year a hundredfold. The LORD blessed him, and the man became rich, and gained more and more until he became very wealthy. (verses 12–13, ESV)

In this challenging new spring, Isaac revealed his trust in God by remaining a man of peace while conflict arose with his neighbors over water rights to various wells (verses 14–33). Isaac eventually moved his camp to a place known as Beersheba, where the Lord provided an overflowing well. Meanwhile, God continued to encourage him:

> And the LORD appeared to him the same night and said, "I am the God of your father Abraham; do not fear, for I am with you. I will bless you and multiply your descendants for My servant Abraham's sake." (verse 24)

And watch Isaac's response:

So he built an altar there and called on the name of the LORD,
and he pitched his tent there. (verse 25)

Isaac was following in his father's footsteps, honoring the Lord for
the blessings of spring and for the rich, ever-new adventure of following
God in the light of His amazing promises.

All in the Family

Then there's the young man Jacob, a son of Isaac and Rebekah, as he
journeyed from his parents and childhood home to a distant land (his
mother's former country, in fact), where he would eventually marry and
father a large family. Along the way under the stars one night, Jacob had
a dream that reached to heaven, and he heard God's voice promising His
presence and blessing in the uncertain years ahead (Genesis 28:10–17).
What an assuring experience for anyone facing the challenges of a new
spring!

Many years later in yet another decisive new spring, Jacob returned
to the homeland of his father Isaac and grandfather Abraham, bringing
along his large family and vast herds that God had blessed him with.
Jacob was following God's guidance in this, but it wasn't an easy transition. Along the way he encountered God again, this time in the form of
an angel who wrestled Jacob through the night hours and then finally
blessed him at dawn (32:22–32). For this new springtime on the horizon,
the wrestling angel gave him a new name—Israel (verse 28). Again we
observe how a new spring can bring us a new and deeper identity.

God reinforced this experience for Jacob shortly afterward and this
time accompanied it with renewed and greater promises in the same vein
as those Abraham and Isaac had received:

God appeared to Jacob again…and blessed him.… Also God said
to him: "I am God Almighty. Be fruitful and multiply; a nation

and a company of nations shall proceed from you, and kings shall
come from your body. The land which I gave Abraham and Isaac
I give to you; and to your descendants after you I give this land."
(35:9–12)

And catch Jacob's response:

So Jacob set up a pillar in the place where He [the Lord] talked
with him, a pillar of stone; and he poured a drink offering on it,
and he poured oil on it. And Jacob called the name of the place
where God spoke with him, Bethel. (verses 14–15)

I hope you're seeing the pattern here of what springtimes can bring—
a renewal of God's promises, a confirmation of a new identity, a refocusing
of future vision and vocation, and a reviving of our worship and reverence
for the Lord. All this can be our experience, in a way that's unique for
each of us, as we let God lead us into our own new beginnings.

Overwhelming Obstacles

This family heritage of springtime blessings continues in the story of the
last major character in the book of Genesis, Jacob's son Joseph. But now
there's a major new element to the pattern (again with wise instruction for
us today). With Joseph, each new springtime seems to lurch suddenly
into tragedy—until out of the pain and hardship and against all odds,
another new spring emerges.

The new pattern began with Joseph's teenage years, when he enjoyed
his father's lavish favor and dreamed of an honorable future (37:1–10).
His older brothers, however, were inflamed with jealousy. They conspired
to kill Joseph, then decided at the last moment to sell him as a slave to
some traders in a passing caravan bound for Egypt (verses 11–36). The
promise of Joseph's youth was extinguished—or so it seemed.

But in Egypt a new spring for Joseph slowly developed. Potiphar, a military official, had purchased the young slave, and Joseph served him with God-given strength and effectiveness—so much so that Potiphar eventually put him in charge of his household (39:1–6). Now everything was looking up.

You remember the story of what happened next. Captivated by Joseph's good looks and commanding presence, Potiphar's wife tried to seduce him; failing at that, she claimed that he'd assaulted her. Caught in her trap, Joseph landed abruptly in the depths of prison (verses 7–20).

Over time, however, his God-inspired wisdom and skills again paid off, even in jail. Another springtime unfolded for him as the warden put Joseph in charge of the other inmates. "And whatever he did, the LORD made it succeed" (verse 23, ESV). After Joseph displayed his remarkable gift from God for interpreting dreams, a pathway to freedom seemed possible (40:1–22). However, time passed, and nothing came of it (40:23).

Finally—suddenly—the moment arrived. Through an amazing connection of circumstances, Joseph was whisked out of prison (after a quick shave and shower and a change of clothes) and brought before Pharaoh himself. There he was asked to interpret his majesty's mystifying dream of the night before. With God's enablement and tactful boldness, Joseph did just that (the dream foretold a long drought for Egypt). Meanwhile he also passed along God's instructions to Pharaoh for how to prepare for the coming ordeal. Pharaoh at once agreed to comply. It must have sent shock waves into every corner of the kingdom when, in the next breath, he appointed Joseph to oversee all the national preparations for the approaching crisis—in a royal position that was second only to Pharaoh himself (41:1–46).

In a matter of hours, Joseph had gone from the obscurity of imprisonment to the highest government office in the world's most powerful nation, with vast authority and responsibilities.

Seldom, if ever, will new springtimes burst so quickly onto the scene for folks like you and me; nevertheless, Joseph's experience has much to teach us. His rise from the depths would never have happened without his integrity, his faithfulness to God and others, his hard work using the skills and gifts God had equipped him with, and his deepening wisdom. These are proven qualities that can open doors—more quickly than we might ever imagine—for God to bring new springtimes our way.

You know the rest of Joseph's story (Genesis 42–50), which amounted to a magnificent opportunity to exert international influence. Joseph rescued his own family from famine, thereby laying the foundation for the emergence of Israel as a nation, all according to God's plan.

It's wise to remember that there's no limit to the new beginnings God can open up to us with each fresh birth of springtime. The way we respond to these opportunities has enormous implications for what follows in our lives. So in the next few chapters, let's reflect on some ways that spring's renewal plays out in the four crucial areas of our identity, our relationships, our roles, and our faith.

Reflect and Respond

1. What do you enjoy most about nature's season of spring? What do you like least about it?

2. How well do you handle change? Do you like to keep things the same, or are you open to change? Why do you think you are like that?

3. How did the springtimes of your childhood and youth affect you? Did they imbue you with confidence and hope for the future? In what ways have you had to overcome the experiences of your childhood and youth?

4. This chapter has highlighted several examples from the book of Genesis of individuals who experienced a spring

season during their adulthood. None of them were overtly seeking such an experience, yet each embraced the opportunity. How would you respond to a midlife or late-in-life call of God to a completely different life?

5. What need, if any, do you sense in your own life for renewal, for new beginnings?

6. If you're in a spring season at this time in your life, what work do you expect this to require from you in the near future?

7

Spring and Our Identity

People can often be misguided about their own identity. Have you ever known a ridiculously talented guy who lacked confidence? Or a beautiful young lady who thought she was ugly? We all know sharp-tongued, judgmental people who leave a trail of carnage in their wake, yet they believe they're dispensing helpful wisdom. And then there are dads (my kids include me here) who erroneously believe their puns are funny.

Yes, we all need help seeing who we really are.

Consider the following words that David declared to God:

My frame was not hidden from You,
When I was made in secret,
And skillfully wrought in the lowest parts of the earth.
Your eyes saw my substance, being yet unformed.
And in Your book they all were written,
The days fashioned for me,
When as yet there were none of them. (Psalm 139:15–16)

What David acknowledges here about himself is true for all of us. But isn't it fascinating that, while God knew us before we were born, some people reside in their own skin for seventy years or more and still don't truly know themselves?

GROWING IN SELF-KNOWLEDGE

Each time we enter a new stage of life, we have the opportunity to learn something about ourselves. We may assume we have a firm grip on our identity, but then we enter college and discover that the morals and religious beliefs our parents tried to instill in us simply don't reflect who we really are. Or we enter parenthood, bringing with us the serene assumption that we're unselfish. But there's nothing like a baby's soiled diaper at three in the morning to provide a fresh perspective on selflessness!

When I first started dating Lisa, she was pretty, vivacious, and the life of the party. She was living on her own and not overly interested in motherhood. In fact, on our first date she informed me that she'd seen a documentary chronicling the pain of childbirth and thus had decided to avoid the experience altogether. Lisa's older sisters worried that she, being a free-spirited, somewhat self-indulgent young woman, was unprepared to make the necessary sacrifices required of good mothers.

But then everything changed. Two years after our wedding, Lisa gave birth to our first child, Mike. He was adorable. Lisa's heart melted. There was absolutely *nothing* she wouldn't do for him. I don't think anyone who knew Lisa as a single adult (including her mother) could have imagined what an amazing, nurturing, lay-down-her-life-for-her-kids mother she would become. Lisa's entry into parenthood disclosed a side of her she didn't know existed.

Spring fosters both dreams and exploration concerning who we are. Childhood commences with perhaps our most important springtime, in which we discover and embrace our identity in a process that takes much time as well as a variety of experiences. That's why it's crucial for children to have time to play with friends and to experiment with a wide array of activities including sports, music, and art. Children begin to discover the pursuits and activities that fit them best.

Unfortunately, some parents think that the most important lesson for their offspring to learn is a strong work ethic. So they march their preteen off to get a paper route or a position at the local store bagging groceries. While other children are reading, making friends, or taking music lessons, these young employees are learning that life consists of hard work.

While it *is* important to develop a robust work ethic, many children's work responsibilities deprived them of going to summer camp or on a family vacation or being involved in sports. They always had to go to work. Often young adults skip college because they already have a decent-paying job and see no immediate need to spend hard-earned money furthering their education. Later in life they find themselves in a full-blown midlife crisis as they realize that since childhood they've been laboring but not really living.

Other parents cling to the belief that their children must learn to stick with commitments regardless of how unpleasant they may be. So they force their daughter to practice the piano for an hour every day, though she long ago lost interest and now begs to play soccer with her friends instead. Of course children do need to understand commitment and the importance of finishing what they start, but it's imperative that they also learn about themselves. Why force your child to do something she hates?

When our daughter was in first grade, we enrolled her in ballet. After a couple of lessons, it was obvious she hated it. After several months she despised it even more. I think she had joined only to get the sparkly outfit. She left the dance studio in tears one afternoon, and we didn't force her to return. She went on to try piano, tap dance, and several other activities and enjoyed them all, but none of them made her heart sing.

Then she discovered figure skating. She fell in love! No more lectures about commitment and perseverance, even when she had 6:30 a.m. practices. (I could have used a few of those lectures myself when I had to drive her to practice and wait in the cold!) Figure skating resonated with her spirit; she had found herself.

This search for self-discovery is why spring is so important, especially when you're young. If as a child you experienced significant moments of nurture as well as a variety of opportunities to achieve success, you may have entered your adult years full of confidence and hope for the future. Conversely, if in the spring of your childhood you suffered denigration, abuse, neglect, or abandonment, you may still be filled with insecurity and fear.

Whether you're a parent, a teacher, a boss, a pastor, or a Brownies leader, you have the ability to nurture or squelch the springtime of others.

THE IMPRESSIONABLE SEASON

In his book *Outliers: The Story of Success,* Malcolm Gladwell relates a landmark study of gifted children by Lewis Terman beginning in 1921.[11] Terman wanted to test the hypothesis that IQ is the greatest determining influence on one's future success: the smarter you are, the more successful you're likely to be in life. The assumption appeared logical enough, but is it true?

To test it, Terman sorted through the records of over 250,000 elementary school children and eventually settled on 1,470 children whose IQs were 140 or higher. This ranked them at the genius level.

Years later, after those children had reached adulthood, Terman revisited 750 of the males and classified them into three groups, based on the degree of "success" they had attained. He found that the highest ranked group "overwhelmingly came from the middle and upper classes. Their homes were filled with books." Moreover, half of them came from homes where the father had a college degree—"an uncommon accomplishment at the time the study was conducted."

This contrasted greatly with the backgrounds of the lowest ranked group, those who had seemingly accomplished the least with their above-average cognitive horsepower. Those in the underachieving group "came from the other side of the tracks. Almost one third of the participants in this group had a parent who had dropped out of school before the eighth grade."[12]

Terman concluded that environment, not genetics, is the single greatest contributing factor to the future success or failure of a child. The parents who instilled in their children a sense of optimism and confidence saw their children enter adulthood better prepared to experience success.

So much of what we become as adults hinges on how well our parents helped us navigate the springtime of our youth.

Consider the fascinating story told in the best-selling book *The Other Wes Moore: One Name, Two Fates* written by (as you might expect) Wes Moore.[13] In December 2000 the *Baltimore Sun* ran separate articles on two young men, both of whom happened to be named Wes Moore. The two men didn't know each other, though they both hailed from the same section of Baltimore. They were both African Americans reared in low-income homes by single mothers, and they were almost the same age. Both had been rebellious teens and had fallen in with bad crowds.

One of the men was in the news for being awarded a Rhodes scholarship. He'd served in Afghanistan as a United States Army captain and was preparing to attend Oxford University. A bright future stretched before him.

The other Wes Moore was in the news after being sentenced to life in prison for his role in an armed robbery during which an off-duty police officer was shot and killed. This young man's future appeared bleak.

Significantly, the father of the first Wes Moore had nurtured him before he died prematurely from disease, and his mother went on to encourage him to better himself through education and hard work. When he showed signs of delinquency, his mother intervened and dispatched him to military school to learn discipline and self-management.

The other Wes Moore had been abandoned as a child and was later mocked and rejected by his father. He grew up in a ghetto environment rife with unemployment and violence that cultivated cynicism for the future.

Receiving encouragement and nurture during our spring seasons can enable the tender saplings in our lives to take root and eventually produce a bountiful harvest.

GRASPING THE POSSIBILITIES

Of course, spring seasons aren't limited to our childhood. As each new spring emerges in life, we have a fresh opportunity to gain insights into our identity and perhaps to reinvent or at least refocus ourselves.

In his book *Decision Points,* George W. Bush describes how his life radically changed in 1986. He and his wife, Laura, had escaped with some friends to the Broadmoor resort in Colorado Springs to celebrate their fortieth birthdays. On the first night George and his friends drank heavily. The next morning as he went for his daily jog, Bush reflected on his embarrassing behavior the night before and on the adverse effects alcohol exerted on him. Returning to his room, he informed Laura that he was giving up drinking alcohol. He reinvented himself. That decision commenced a new season in his life. Ten years later he was governor of Texas and later the president of the United States.

When spring arrives in our lives, we have a fresh opportunity to grasp the possibilities God places before us and to become the people He created us to be.

I have the privilege of working with an organization that ministers to Christian CEOs in corporate America. One of them, Steve, retired a decade ago as the president of a large, publicly traded company. He was a typical hard-driving businessman, leading a major multinational company. Today Steve admits he was not the husband or father he should have been back then. Though well-intentioned, he was extremely busy and regularly away from home. Compounding the problem, his priorities were misplaced.

After a successful career, Steve entered retirement early, and a new spring season arrived. What would he do with it? Would he embrace the next stage of his life with the same drive and determination that had characterized his career? He now had three granddaughters. Would he relate to them in the same manner as he had to his only daughter? Or would he use this new spring to reinvent himself?

Today, by his own admission, Steve is a different man. At the outset of his retirement years, he performed major "spring cleaning" in his spiritual life. He also refurbished his relationships with his wife and daughter. Today his granddaughters are the joy of his life. He currently mentors other CEOs, teaching them what he learned the hard way. Steve has used his new spring season to embrace new possibilities for his life and to free himself from some harmful habits.

Interestingly, as Steve entered retirement, he interviewed twenty CEOs who had recently retired. He asked them, "What has changed since your retirement?" Their most common responses were: (1) I've lost my purpose; (2) I've lost my identity; (3) I've lost my security; (4) I didn't realize how far I'd drifted away in my relationships with God and my wife; (5) I didn't realize the degree of maladjustments my spouse had to make to keep our marriage together.

Entering a new spring can rattle our identity. But times of change also provide the opportunity to mature into wiser, kinder, and more successful people than we were before.

REFLECT AND RESPOND

1. How have new stages of your life helped you to learn something new about your identity?

2. Have you ever assumed something about yourself that you later discovered to be false? If so, what was it? Do others assume things about you that are not true?

3. Think about how you typically respond to change. How much of this reaction is rooted in your self-identity?

4. Have you taken much time in your life to try new things or to explore new possibilities? If not, what is one specific assumption about yourself that it would be wise to examine and reconsider at this time in your life? Do you sense you may have missed out on some important things because you failed to pursue your dreams in spring?

8

Our Relationships in Spring

Relationships come in seasons. While some people enjoy lifelong friendships, each new stage of life provides both the opportunity and the incentive to develop new relationships. We arrive at a new school and initiate a conversation with the student sitting at the desk beside us, having no idea he'll become our best friend through high school. We meet our college roommate with no inkling she'll one day be a bridesmaid at our wedding. We begin our new job or join a new church or move to a retirement community and stand at the threshold of an entirely new world of relationships with multifaceted possibilities.

Proverbs 13:20 shows us how we take on the characteristics of those we spend time with: "Whoever walks with the wise becomes wise, but the companion of fools will suffer harm" (ESV). (That principle ought to provide a sobering afterthought for those whose favorite companion is their pet!) Think of the enormous potential contained within each relationship. New friendships are especially common in spring, so every time we enter a new stage of life—attending a new school, moving to a new location, beginning a new job, starting a new stage of parenting—we ought to keep our eyes open for friends who could enhance our lives.

Shortly after Lisa and I were married, we moved to Fort Worth, Texas, to attend graduate school. In our days as single college students, we'd both enjoyed active social lives. But after we relocated fifteen hundred miles away, my fanatical buddies who used to play pickup hockey with me every day after classes were gone. Lisa had left her beloved sisters and her three best friends and moved to a state where she could barely comprehend the strong drawls of the Southern gals. We realized we needed new friends!

One weekend we attended a party for young couples at an acquaintance's home. All the women congregated in the living room and began chatting energetically. The men, quite naturally, strategically migrated to the dining room, where the food was located.

I met lots of people that evening, including a guy named Lou. He was interesting and had a great sense of humor. We talked nonstop. At a certain point we both realized we should probably mingle and meet other people. So we did. Before long, however, we ended up back in a huddle together. (It could have been a mutual fascination or the fact that neither of us ever strayed far from the dessert platters!) Finally we realized the evening had passed and neither of us had any idea what our wives were doing. We both sheepishly made our way over to the sea of women spread out across the large living room.

After I spied Lisa sitting in a corner talking excitedly to someone I'd never met, I pointed out my wife to Lou. He explained that the woman my wife was talking to was his wife. In a house filled with dozens of people, Lisa and I had simultaneously connected with the same couple at opposite ends of the house. A great friendship commenced.

THE RICHNESS OF VARIETY

Think about each stage of life you've experienced thus far: your childhood, elementary school, high school, college, various jobs, new parenthood, middle age, and retirement. Recall the friends and colleagues who were the most meaningful to you during each of these stages. Were they the same people over the years? Your closest friends may have changed over time. Perhaps as you changed schools, jobs, or neighborhoods, or maybe as you grew and matured, you began looking for different kinds of friends. As you entered parenthood or advanced in your career, your lifestyle called for a different type of relationship. It wasn't that you no longer liked your old friends; it's just that as your life changed, so did your relationships.

Some people insist on following the same script every time. Just like the man who cannot bear to deviate from meat and potatoes every night for dinner, some people keep the same handful of buddies their entire lives or at least gravitate constantly to the same kind of friends. But if variety is the spice of life, then diversity in friends greatly enriches the quality of our existence.

Lisa excels at this. Throughout the years, no matter where we've moved, she's managed to collect a rather odd assortment of companions. She has always been attracted to slightly (okay, more than slightly) quirky friends.

When I finished graduate school, I began my first job as a church minister. This transition launched us into an entirely new stage of life. It was the first time we'd developed friendships while occupying the role of a minister and minister's wife. It was then that I really started to notice Lisa's propensity to acquire unique friends.

There was Wanda, a carefree, cheerful woman who was always laughing and doing zany things. One day she and Lisa went to Wal-Mart and decided to shop separately. Lisa asked how she would know when Wanda was ready to leave.

"Oh, you'll know," Wanda replied mysteriously.

Sure enough, as Lisa was roaming the aisles, she suddenly heard her name bellowed from the other side of the massive store: "Liiisaaa! Time to go!"

Lisa embarrassedly scampered as quickly as possible toward her friend at the front of the store while every shopper's eye was seemingly fixed on her.

As Wanda went to pay for her purchases, the checkout clerk awkwardly informed her that her credit card had been declined. "Hand me the phone!" Wanda bellowed. She called the 800 number on the back of the card and commanded: "Up my limit!" They did.

Lisa's friends included Vonne, a delightful single mom who became a dear friend and was invited to all of our holiday occasions.

There was also Margaret, a kind, gentle woman who suffered from a genetic birth defect, which meant that her cognitive abilities equated to that of a young teen, but her tender spirit and lively sense of humor were a balm for Lisa. She insisted on sitting beside Lisa in church every Sunday.

And there was Karen, a fellow shopaholic, who was always a lot of fun though occasionally a little irreverent. Karen and her husband, Mark, had a great marriage, and she provided Lisa a role model.

And then there was Lisa's friend Mumzy—perhaps the wackiest widow I've ever met. She always leaves you gasping for air as she relates her latest hilarious adventure. A classic "Mumzyism" is the time she was housesitting for a friend in Canada. At 2:30 one morning she awoke and went to the kitchen to get something to drink. That's when the dog indicated it needed to go outside, where it was twenty-five degrees below zero. In the process of the innocuous act of taking the dog out, the cat escaped, and Mumzy accidentally locked herself out of the house, wearing nothing but a thin nightgown and slippers.

She saw lights on in a neighboring house that was supposed to be abandoned but allegedly was being used as a drug house. She hurried to the door and knocked, but no one answered. (If they had, the sight of her might have been enough to shock the nefarious lawbreakers out of their life of crime!)

Mumzy walked several blocks in the frigid Canadian night to a gas station, where she inadvertently terrified the young attendant who was counting the day's receipts in the back office.

And that's one of the tamer Mumzy stories!

Can you imagine the life you lead when you have a collection of friends like that around you?

What to Look for in Friends

Life isn't meant to be boring, but it probably will be if you surround yourself with people just like yourself.

The most popular or respected people in your office, school, neighborhood, or church don't necessarily make the best friends. Look for the people who love life, not those who love money or their status or their accomplishments. Choose friends who have the most wisdom, not necessarily the most possessions. Life's too short to surround yourself with people who bring you down or hold you back.

Choose to associate with people who have a *joie de vivre*…and you'll soon have it too.

Reflect and Respond

1. What are the most important factors you look for in choosing friends?

2. How open are you to forming new friendships? When was the last time you made a friend?

3. What are some things you could do at this time to actively pursue forming new friendships in your life?

4. How diverse would you say your friends are? Is it possible that the range of your friendships is too narrow? Are you bored with your current friends?

5. Is someone close to you in a spring season at this time? How could you encourage that person with something you've learned so far from this book?

9

Our Roles in Spring

Spring is what prevents us from descending into dreary predictability and stagnation. It allows us to attempt new things and to develop and exercise additional skills. It keeps life fresh.

In Charles Dickens's classic work *A Christmas Carol,* the miserly Ebenezer Scrooge mistakenly assumes that his sole role in life is that of a businessman (and a ruthless one at that). Long ago he became stuck in that identity, bypassing life's pleasures along the way. He almost misses the exhilarating and rewarding new roles that await him.

Fortunately, as the story goes, spring comes at last, even for Ebenezer.

A Progression of Roles

God will keep bringing new springs into our lives as we enter new stages of life, and each one usually comes with a new role for us to assume.

Our first major role is simply that of being a child. For many, this is a carefree, joyous time. For others, it's like walking through a minefield.

Later we start attending school, and we take on the major role of student—a role that will constantly evolve as the years go by. Later still come our roles as employees, husbands or wives, parents, grandparents, and many more. We may take on various roles in service and ministry through our churches, as volunteers in organizations, or as managers, executives, or even owners at our places of work. Each role will be different; each will call upon new aspects of our identity and skills.

Not every role you hold will be equally rewarding or successful. You may have had a difficult childhood, or you may not have excelled in school. I've known a lot of bright people who were convinced they were stupid because of how they performed in the classroom. Albert Einstein was perhaps one of the most underrated students in history. He failed physics in college and was labeled a "lazy dog" by a professor. The only class Elvis Presley failed in school was music.

Our modern school system largely focuses on measuring particular behavior as well as specific forms of intelligence as identified on IQ tests. However, specialists such as author and psychologist Howard Gardner of Harvard University highlight the existence of multiple intelligences.[14] Gardner argues that IQ tests measure only one form of intelligence, when in fact there are many. He identifies eight main forms of human intelligence, including *bodily/kinesthetic* intelligence, the ability to accomplish extraordinary physical feats, such as Babe Ruth excelling at baseball. There's also *linguistic* intelligence, in which people have a strong aptitude for learning and using languages. And there's *spatial* intelligence, a sense of direction and the ability to navigate. I again think of Albert Einstein, who could calculate the positions of galaxies on the back of a used envelope but had to get directions from his office to his house nearby.[15] There's also *interpersonal* intelligence, which involves people skills. We all know people who are brilliant with book learning but hopelessly inept in social settings.

Meanwhile another psychologist and author, Daniel Goleman, has written a great deal on *emotional* intelligence. He notes that while IQ scores are generally highlighted when people graduate from college, emotional intelligence is more likely to determine outstanding job performance.[16] Individuals who excel at working with people or at problem solving often leave traditional schools doubting their own intelligence because they performed poorly on a standard IQ test. Some brilliantly creative people wrongly conclude that because their reading comprehension is poor or because they never mastered long division, they must be idiots.

The beauty of entering a new spring is that it provides the opportunity to take on new roles that better draw upon our natural intelligence and aptitude. I'm a firstborn child. My parents, like many others, assumed that their first child would dethrone Einstein as the prodigy of the ages. If you asked my mother, she would proudly inform you that her brilliant boy wonder learned to speak almost before leaving the hospital. In her revisionist history, I was already doing household chores at age two and was reading Shakespeare by age four. So you can imagine my parents' shock when my kindergarten teacher tried to *flunk* me! (So much for updating the theory of relativity.)

Later, in the eleventh grade, I was struggling in French. There were three French teachers at my high school; I had the misfortune of ending up with the most demanding of the three, every year. My problems were compounded by the disconcerting fact that she never spoke a word of English in class. One day she posed a question to me in French that was hopelessly beyond my meager comprehension. I timidly (and foolishly) gave a feeble answer, to which my teacher replied (in English this time, so I would understand), "Richard Blackaby, you have a *fungus* for a brain!" Not exactly a confidence booster for someone who was already pondering whether he had what it took to enter university.

Not surprisingly, my lack of language aptitude seems to be shared by my children. My son Daniel's eighth-grade French teacher arbitrarily transferred him from French into law class halfway through the semester without consulting him. When Daniel asked why he'd been transferred, his teacher replied, "Daniel, haven't the French already suffered enough?"

As I neared high school graduation, I had little confidence in my academic ability. But then I entered university, and something quite unexpected occurred. I began doing well! I was able to redefine myself in my new role as a college student (one that didn't require French). My success was a delight to me—and a surprise to those who had known me in high school.

Then I entered graduate school and established myself in a role that allowed me to focus even more narrowly on subjects that interested me. I later earned a PhD, became president of a graduate school, and have written numerous books.

So it is that spring draws upon our identity and our passions—while sometimes also providing us an opportunity to prove that our schoolteachers were mistaken.

CHANGING THINGS UP

Suppose you graduate from high school at age eighteen, then work at a full-time job for forty-seven years until you retire at age sixty-five. By your retirement, you'll have worked approximately ninety-four thousand hours. Imagine that during all those hours, you perform the same role at the identical workplace. Regardless of the task, that's a lot of time to be doing the same thing.

Thankfully God periodically leads us to change things up!

Remember, God created us to experience seasons. He invented diversity! Each spring brings with it the invitation to embrace a new assignment. While some people work their entire adult lives for the same company (rarely in the same job), most of us assume numerous roles over the course of our lives.

Diane was married at age nineteen and had her first child when she was twenty. She embraced motherhood and threw her considerable energy into homemaking and bringing up her two boys. But when her second son was in high school, Diane, still in her thirties, realized that her child-rearing stage of life was drawing to a close. So she decided to become a nurse.

At that point she entered a new springtime. She lacked the necessary high school science credits to enter a nursing program, so she returned to high school. She was in the same science classes as her teenage son (they were lab partners). She then moved to a large city to attend university and shared an apartment with her now-college-age son, while commuting for two hours back home to her husband on weekends. (As I said, she's a high-energy woman!)

Diane went on to become an outstanding nurse who eventually filled a top management position in the local hospital. Today, in retirement, she's embracing her new role as a grandmother (and having a blast).

George Dawson became a poster child for yet another spring. Born in 1898, he never learned to read as a child and spent the first ninety-eight years of his life illiterate. Upon learning about a local adult education program, Dawson enrolled, learned to read, and went on to earn his GED at age 103. He wrote his life story, *Life Is So Good,* and was interviewed on television by Oprah Winfrey. A school was even named after him. Dawson demonstrated that we're never too old to see a new spring blossom in our lives.

There's always another spring on the horizon. Even as we enter retirement, God has far more in store for us than merely playing golf and bridge at a country club! The psalmist gives us a better picture: "Those who are planted in the house of the LORD shall flourish in the courts of our God. They shall still bear fruit in old age; they shall be fresh and flourishing" (Psalm 92:13–14). God knows how we can thrive in every stage of life.

How Many Springs Can One Man Have?

Melvin Wells may have set a modern-day record for the number of springs in one person's lifetime. He was born into a hardworking family in Kansas. However, his childhood came to a screeching halt when his father died prematurely. Melvin, an only child, became the man of the house.

When the Great Depression descended like a black cloak over the Midwest, Melvin hitched a ride on a train headed for Chicago in search of an elusive job. He eventually married a beautiful young nurse he'd met at a soda shop, then moved on to Tulsa, Oklahoma, where he found work at a Sears, Roebuck and Co. store. Here he settled into one of the most active stages of his life. He was good at his job and was soon earning a comfortable living. His wife, Carrie, worked as a scrub nurse at the local hospital, and they welcomed two daughters and a son into their growing household.

But there was something about Melvin that periodically caused him to grow restless. It wasn't that he couldn't hold a job; he was always good at what he did. Rather, after a period of time, he would begin to sense that a new spring was approaching and that his life was about to change.

When his children were teenagers, Melvin packed up his family and moved to Los Angeles. His family formed the nucleus of a new church. He found a job at another Sears, Roebuck, and Co. store and was soon managing its most successful department. He put his three children through college and saw each of them get married and start families.

Then Melvin and Carrie began to sense once again that a new spring was coming. This time they didn't just move across the country. They took early retirement and set off for Lusaka, Zambia, as associate missionaries. They ran a home that cared for children of missionaries who worked deep in the bush. Melvin, a born salesman, promoted a correspondence course all over Zambia. (He would boldly enter local taverns and sign up all the patrons for a course on the life of Christ.) He also tended the finest garden in the country, although the snakes were nasty. Though technically retired at this stage of their lives, Melvin and Carrie were living in Africa, traveling around the world, making amazing friends, and having the time of their lives.

But then winter descended on that stage of their lives as well. They moved back to a gated community in the Los Angeles area to retire (again). Never one to sit idle, Melvin was soon responsible for overseeing the swimming pool and community center in his housing complex. He also took a part-time job at a major newspaper. He would call on customers who had canceled their subscriptions and try to convince them to resubscribe. Having lost none of his salesmanship over the years, he soon set records for resubscriptions, and his supervisor asked him to record his techniques so the newspaper could use them to train others.

To make life even more interesting, their oldest grandson moved in with them as a teenager and enrolled in the local high school. A new stage of life was well under way.

After several years Melvin and Carrie began to sense that they wouldn't remain in California. Melvin's mother in Kansas was widowed for the second time and needed her son's help. (This feisty lady was still canning preserves at age 100 and lived to be 106.) So Melvin and Carrie left their quaint retirement community in Southern California and moved to northeast Oklahoma, across the state line from Melvin's mother in Kansas. Now octogenarians, they joined a church, and Melvin was soon the Sunday school superintendent, a deacon, and an active volunteer in his church's hospital visitation ministry. Then he was asked to be a state representative for the AARP. At age 81, Melvin bought his first computer so he could keep up with his voluminous correspondence.

Melvin always preferred driving brand-new cars with oversized tires because he claimed you never knew when you might need a passing gear. He put that gear to good use for the next decade as he commuted to Kansas to check on his mother, drove to Tulsa for state AARP meetings, and sped to Joplin, Missouri, to get a "good deal." (No one ever derived as much pleasure as Melvin did from getting the seniors' discount at McDonalds.) His life was full and seemingly as busy as ever.

Then winter set in once again. His bride of sixty years died, and for the first time in more than half a century, Melvin was alone.

That didn't last long. At age 87, Melvin still possessed a striking appearance. He was tall, with a full head of white hair, a quick clip to his gait, and a salesman's charming smile. Every widow in the church was smitten and soon bringing him casseroles and homemade pies. Melvin was pushing 90 and had just entered a new spring! At 88, he married Lillian, and they began an enjoyable new life together.

It wasn't until Melvin was well into his nineties that his health began to deteriorate. Some wondered if his energy would ever abate; ultimately, it did. Eventually he moved into a nursing home. Early one morning a nurse found him on the floor beside his bed. It appeared he'd been trying to get out of bed when he died. I like to think that Melvin—my grandpa—saw the angels coming to usher him into a wonderful new, eternal springtime, and—as impatient as ever—he had eagerly started climbing out of bed to join them.

The truth is, even death is not the final season. There's a spectacular new spring—more glorious than any we've experienced on earth—that awaits those who have heaven as their ultimate destiny.

REFLECT AND RESPOND

1. What are the most important roles in your life at this time? In which ones, if any, are you presently experiencing a spring season, a time of new beginnings? In which roles are you most in *need* of new beginnings to overcome possible stagnation?

2. As you reflect on your past, what are the most significant new roles that have come into your life? What was it like for you to launch into these? What fears, if any, did you experience?

3. What further opportunities, if any, do you see opening up for you in the major roles in your life?

4. How open are you to accepting new roles in your life at this time?

10

Spring and Our Faith

Our faith is meant to be dynamic, not static. Each new stage of life unveils unique possibilities for our faith to grow and for us to gain new insights and experiences related to God's character.

The Bible relates numerous examples of this. Here are just a few:

- *Abraham* was a successful businessman in Mesopotamia when, as we observed earlier, God instructed him to leave his home and travel to an unfamiliar country (Genesis 12:1). By faith the aged patriarch did what God told him to, and over the course of his amazing spiritual pilgrimage, he became a "friend of God" (James 2:23).

- *Jacob* was a deceitful brother who robbed his twin of his inheritance and brazenly lied to his father. Then, while fleeing to another country, he had a life-changing encounter with God that we briefly examined earlier. On this occasion Jacob exclaimed, "Surely the LORD is in this place, and I did not know it" (Genesis 28:16). Thus would begin Jacob's journey of faith that would lead him to become a revered patriarch of God's people.

- *Moses* had been shepherding his father-in-law's sheep in the wilderness for forty years when God ushered him into a spring season (Exodus 3) that radically changed his life and his walk with God—and miraculously delivered a nation out of slavery.

- *Peter, Andrew, James,* and *John* were busy at their fishermen's trade when Jesus stood on the shore and beckoned them to follow Him (Mark 1:16–20). Those four men could never have imagined what a spectacular new season they were entering when they left their familiar fishing boats.

These people were adults, well established in their homes, jobs, and lifestyles. But as they entered a new spring season, they experienced God as never before.

Abraham believed in God before, but through his odyssey to a promised land, he learned firsthand that God can take a childless centenarian and make him the father of a multitude.

Jacob may have thought he'd burned every bridge to success, but he came to understand that God could transform a "Jacob" (meaning "cheater" or "he who supplants") into an "Israel" (meaning "God strives" or "God rules").

Moses may have assumed his failures disqualified him from helping anyone, but after he left his flock and returned to Egypt, he discovered that all things are possible with God.

Those four fishermen may have been pious businessmen, but when they left their nets to follow Jesus, God turned their world upside down.

God doesn't always ask us to change careers or to relocate to another country before He shows us fascinating new facets about His character. However, it's often as we enter a new spring season that we're in the best position to go deeper in our relationship with God.

I previously explained this phenomenon in a book titled *Unlimiting God: Increasing Your Capacity to Experience the Divine.*[17] In it I looked at the ways many Christians inadvertently limit what they know and experience of God because they remain cocooned in a safe, predictable, manageable life. As a result, they never advance beyond a shallow relationship with God.

Occasionally God will introduce a new spring into our lives so we can experience deeper dimensions in our walk with Him. We take on a job that's way over our heads, and we desperately cry out to God for help. Or we move to an unfamiliar state or country, and God's provision and sufficiency becomes clear in ways we never experienced before. We might suffer a grave illness or endure a tragedy or become a parent, and suddenly God grabs our attention to a greater degree.

Every time you enter a new springtime, prepare yourself for the brand-new work God may do in your life.

Of all the people I've known, my father is probably the best example of this truth.

Obeying the Call

Henry Blackaby was born in Williams Lake, British Columbia. (My dad always adds, "Not in the lake but in the town.") His father was a Brit who raised his three boys in a proper English manner.

My dad is by nature a shy introvert, and throughout his youth he never demonstrated an aptitude for public speaking. Yet as a teenager Dad sensed God calling him to enter Christian ministry. Upon graduating from university, he took a bold step. He left Canada and traveled to San Francisco to enroll in seminary. Thus began a new spring season in his life.

Living eight hundred miles from home, Dad adjusted to this foreign culture. (Good heavens, they ate fried chicken without a knife and fork!) His time as a student in San Francisco coincided with the hippie movement.

While in school he met and eventually married my mother (an American and over-the-top extrovert). There were no churches from my father's denomination in the area, so he joined a church from a different tradition. This shift in denominations would prove fortuitous. He entered a network of churches far larger than anything he'd known before.

A small church eventually hired him to be their part-time music minister. When the minister of education resigned, the church gave him that position as well. When the senior pastor retired, the church voted him into that job too. (I suppose my father will be forever grateful that the leader of the women's missionary group remained in office throughout his tenure.) Talk about a trial by fire! The church was in a crime-riddled neighborhood in the Bay Area. In the five years he served that church, Dad performed hundreds of funerals. The police called him several times to help with domestic violence cases. (In one instance he took a gun out of the hands of an enraged husband who had vowed to kill his captive wife.)

Later he was called to a congregation in Los Angeles that was a bit safer. The mayor and city sheriff were members. Challenges continued, however, as the Watts riots occurred during this period.

FURTHER STRETCHING

During his eleven years in California, Dad's understanding of God greatly matured. (He also fathered four sons during those faith-challenging years, the likes of which were enough to drive anyone to become a man of prayer!) You would think that as a respected pastor in a growing church, he was in a perfect place to stay for good, with plenty of opportunities to continue learning and experiencing more of God.

But it became clear to my parents that God was orchestrating a new spring in their lives. A tiny church in Saskatoon, Canada, asked if he would become their pastor, concluding that if he didn't accept, they would have to disband.

Why, you might wonder, would God take my father away from a "successful" ministry to one that appeared to be dying? Others asked the same thing. One pastor drove a hundred miles to dissuade Dad from relocating to Canada. Nevertheless, my parents sensed that a stage of their life was passing and that they faced a new spring season. They accepted the pastorate in Saskatoon. And despite all the amazing experiences of their ministry in California and all they had learned of God and His ways, this new endeavor would stretch their faith to entirely new levels.

Could God have continued to teach my father divine truths while he remained in his comfortable life in Los Angeles? Certainly. But God often uses the changing seasons of our lives to introduce us to new truths we might not otherwise learn.

After my family moved north, Dad immediately recognized that numerous small towns across that vast province of Saskatchewan needed a church. Yet his new congregation in Saskatoon couldn't afford to pay him as their pastor, let alone support the planting of other congregations. Despite this lack of visible funding over the next dozen years, his little flock started dozens of new churches and mission sites. Without any funds from mission agencies, the tiny congregation had to rely on God to provide the resources required to plant churches as far as five hundred miles away. They learned that God often calls people to attempt things that are impossible without His help. But it's only as we obey His leading that we truly *experience* God.

EXPERIENCING GOD

After twelve years in Saskatoon, Dad's denomination asked him to move to Vancouver, British Columbia, and oversee its churches in that region. Throughout the next six years, God continued to work powerfully and to teach my father more about the God he was serving.

Another move to a new position took him to Atlanta (the hub of Delta Air Lines, with whom he would rack up three million air miles). This relocation provided him greater freedom to travel the world, sharing with others what God had taught him.

My father was asked to write about major lessons he'd learned in his ministry, and he did so in his book *Experiencing God: Knowing and Doing the Will of God*. He was fifty-five when it was published, and its vast and enthusiastic reception propelled him into a new stage of life he couldn't have imagined during his years as a pastor serving on a difficult mission field.

But God wasn't through teaching and growing my father. During the next two decades, God took him around the world as well as to the White House, the Pentagon, and the United Nations. Henry Blackaby has spoken to enormous audiences, and he and my mom have met amazing people.

What impresses me the most about my dad's life journey is how God seemed to be constantly teaching him something new. Every succeeding stage in life has been a fresh opportunity for God to take him to deeper levels in his Christian faith. If you ask him, "Henry, what has God been teaching you lately?" he always has fresh and exciting things to share. (I've learned to ask with pen and paper handy so I can glean a new sermon series.)

That's what the springs of life are for. They're God's means of introducing us to amazing new insights into His character and power.

FROM LAUNCHING TO LABOR

Spring is about beginnings. It's the doorstep to each new stage of life. Our compelling question at this stage should be, "During this new season in my life, how might I further develop my identity, relationships, role, and faith?"

How we launch into spring dramatically affects what we experience in summer. If spring is the entryway, summer is the workroom where the majority of the labor occurs. Summer is the season of work and growth, and it's to that season we'll turn next.

REFLECT AND RESPOND

1. In your life at this time, is your faith growing and dynamic? Or is it static and stale?

2. How have new stages in your life helped you to grow deeper in your faith?

3. On a scale of one to ten, how would you rate the way you've handled the springs of your life thus far?

4. In what ways might you be limiting your capacity to experience God more closely and powerfully? What can you do to change this?

5. What is one characteristic of God, such as His power or forgiveness, that you would like to experience to a greater degree? Take a moment to pray and ask God to take you to a deeper knowledge and experience of Him in that area. Then keep your spiritual eyes open for what He introduces into your life next!

11

SUMMER: THE TIME FOR WORK AND GROWTH

Late in 1942, when the Second World War was already three years old, Allied troops gained a hard-fought triumph over General Rommel's Axis forces at El Alamein in North Africa. This followed a prolonged period marked mostly by demoralizing setbacks for the Allies, especially for their ground forces. "Now, however, we have a new experience," observed Winston Churchill in a speech in London. "We have victory—a remarkable and definite victory."

Churchill then went on to add these famous words: "Now this is not the end. It is not even the beginning of the end. But it is, perhaps, the end of the beginning."

The prime minister's remarks serve well as a description of the summers God brings into our lives. Summer is far from the end, yet it's no longer the beginning. We've moved from the excitement of the start-up to a new stage marked by labor and growth. In fact, it's probably good here to recall another statement from that speech of Churchill's, as he reminded everyone that "I have never promised anything but blood, tears, toil, and sweat." Summer, more than any other season, is the time for hard work.

The Picture for Us in Nature

Spring receives a lot of hype, but summer is also exhilarating and is many people's favorite season. When people find out I grew up in Canada, knowing the summers there can be brief, they often ask what Canadians like to do during summer. I reply with a stock Canadian answer: "Well, if it falls on a Saturday, we hold a picnic." Summers are precious, and no one wants to waste them.

Summer is associated with warmth, sunshine, and abundant activity. Once seeds have been planted, summer is a time of growth and maturation. This season's sunshine and rain, in proper amounts, will cause stalks of grain to rapidly stretch heavenward. Meanwhile spring-born animals and birds will gain strength and maturity.

Though it's a season of labor, that work is often made harder by the rising temperatures that sap our strength. During the height of summer, the heat radiates off the earth, baking everything like a convection oven warming a Thanksgiving Day turkey. It seems that the only things invigorated by the heat are the swarms of insects.

Summer days are long and productive. In northern latitudes, evenings can stretch out deliciously, as the sun might not set until ten or eleven o'clock. The sounds of hammers and heavy machinery fill the air as workers capitalize on the extra hours of natural light to build and renovate.

Part of summer's mystique is the knowledge that it's fleeting. "Make hay while the sun shines" is an adage originating perhaps as early as the fifteen hundreds and refers to the fact that heat and sunshine are necessary to turn grass into hay. If livestock are going to have hay in the winter, summer must produce it. God's creatures know instinctively that summer is a time to prepare for winter. As the writer of Proverbs noted, "The ants are a people not strong, yet they prepare their food in summer" (30:25).

Like spring, summer has its dark side. The same radiant rays of sunshine that draw tourists to beaches can also scorch crops and damage skin. Insects torment both livestock and people. Where I grew up, the mosquito was considered the unofficial provincial bird! (There's almost nothing more irritating than trying to sleep at night and hearing the high-pitched whine of a mosquito hovering in anticipation above your head.) Spectacular lightning storms may sporadically strike at the end of a hot summer day and ignite ravenous forest fires that spread rapidly in the heat and dryness. Hailstorms can devastate crops in moments. Heat waves cause death, especially among the poor and the elderly.

THE PICTURE FOR US IN SCRIPTURE

The labor of summer is what the motivating excitement of spring is meant to lead to. Springtime's thrill yields to summer's toil.

In every stage of our lives, including every endeavor, calling, pursuit, relationship, project, and plan, there's always a summer stage—a time for labor or, as Ecclesiastes 3:3 expresses it, "a time to build up."

The work is there to do, and we are designed to do it. This is continually true about us because we're made in God's image, and God Himself is a worker, a craftsman, a builder, and maker. We see this in the Genesis account of creation, of course, as well as in the personified description of those same events in Proverbs 8:22–31, where God's wisdom plays the role in creation of "a master craftsman" (verse 30).

We see it also in the New Testament, where we are described as "His *workmanship,* created in Christ Jesus for *good works,* which God *prepared* beforehand that we should walk in them" (Ephesians 2:10). The picture is clear: God Himself has labored and crafted and prepared on our behalf so that we too can work. Our labor is in response to His.

Today, God is still at work. He continues His dynamic, purposeful activity on our behalf, for His word tells us, "It is God who *works* in you both to will and to do for His good pleasure" (Philippians 2:13). Here again we see that God's labor enables ours, because God's activity is the reason Paul tells believers to "*work out* your own salvation with fear and trembling" (verse 12). We simply can't escape the biblical imperatives that call everyone to engage in attentive, conscientious, purposeful labor.

Sometimes we might think of our work as a necessary evil or at best a sideline activity that, however time demanding, exists only to make possible (and foot the bill for) life's more important and enjoyable pursuits. We might even soothingly remind ourselves of the biblical fact that, after all, humanity's original home was a pleasurable garden, not a factory or a farm. But let's look more closely at that. We read in Genesis 2:15 how "the LORD God took the man and put him in the garden of Eden *to tend and keep it.*" So a working role was the express purpose behind Adam's presence in the garden in the first place. Eden was a workplace, not a resort.

God, in His wisdom, created us for labor—though in this fallen world we often resist that design (along with a great deal more of God's intentions). That's why we so often need encouragement and exhortation to persevere in our tasks, labors, and efforts.

This encouragement and exhortation are exactly what we receive throughout the Scriptures. Returning to Ecclesiastes, we find this reminder: "There is nothing better for a person than that he should eat and drink and find enjoyment in his *toil*. This...is from the hand of God" (2:24, ESV). Enjoyment of our toil may not always come naturally to us, but it can be ours through God's grace. For Scripture exhorts us to "rejoice in his *labor*—this is the gift of God" (5:19). Because of labor's value, we're admonished, "Whatever your hand finds to do, *do it* with your might" (9:10).

That last admonition is echoed in the New Testament. "Whatever you do," Paul says, "*work heartily,* as for the Lord and not for men" (Colossians 3:23, ESV). We're also taught to shun "idleness" (2 Thessalonians 3:6, 11, ESV) and to "not become sluggish" (Hebrews 6:12).

Paul himself exemplifies this God-inspired hard work of summer. After outlining for the Colossians his calling and task, Paul added, "For this I *toil,* struggling with all his energy that he powerfully works within me" (1:29, ESV). He testified that his experience of God's astonishing grace meant that he "*labored* more abundantly…yet not I, but the grace of God which was with me" (1 Corinthians 15:10). He humbly reminded the Thessalonian believers of how he and his coworkers had "*worked* with *labor* and *toil* night and day" (2 Thessalonians 3:8). Paul never slacked off when the task was tough.

This diligence was doubtless a big part of Paul's thoughts as he counseled believers to "join in following my example" (Philippians 3:17). Whenever our summertimes roll around and our tasks lie before us, we would do well to heed Paul's example.

The payoff for all this effort we're called to is truly exceptional. "In *all labor* there is profit" (Proverbs 14:23), and this "profit," in benefits and blessings, will show up in many forms.

It means, for instance, that we participate in the training and discipline that God's fatherly wisdom brings our way. Hard work, to state the obvious, is hard, and that very hardship is essential in God's intricate and sovereign design for our personal transformation and growth.

It also means an opportunity to learn perseverance—patient endurance—which is a priceless treasure. The hardship of our labor "produces perseverance; and perseverance, character; and character, hope" (Romans 5:3–4). The stamina and determination we learn in hard labor will open doors to unimaginable rewards and gains, all from the hand of "the God of patience" (15:5).

Summer is often when we round a corner or crest a hill and discover how much farther we have to go in the course we embarked on so energetically in spring. In those moments we need to hear the Bible's stirring exhortation: "Let us run with *endurance* the race that is set before us" (Hebrews 12:1). "For you have need of endurance," this same book of Hebrews tells us, "so that after you have done the will of God, you may receive the promise" (10:36). It's another way of saying that endurance in summer is what produces an abundant harvest in the fall.

Hard work also brings extra motivation for embracing our privilege of prayer, as the demands of our labor compel us to realize our need for help. We learn to practice active prayer and prayerful action. Therefore we "come boldly to the throne of grace, that we may obtain mercy and find grace to help in time of need" (Hebrews 4:16), and such a "time of need" seems to pop up again and again in our summers.

A CLASSIC BIBLICAL EXAMPLE

The Bible offers countless examples of people experiencing the summer season with its accompanying labor. Nehemiah was a Jewish captive in exile, and his heart was deeply burdened for his homeland of Israel and for the city of Jerusalem, whose ruined walls left her defenseless. An amazing new springtime opened up for Nehemiah when God answered his prayers (Nehemiah 1:4–11) and gave him the opportunity to go to Jerusalem (2:1–8) and lead the effort to rebuild the demolished walls.

Arriving in Jerusalem, Nehemiah went into summer mode. He quietly inspected the entire scene (verses 9–16) to determine what needed to be done. (That kind of preparation is always a strong foundation for our summer labor.) He recognized that the endeavor before him represented "what my God had put in my heart to do" (verse 12). (That's the perfect description of our summer labor.)

As a gifted leader, Nehemiah shared his perspective on the divinely inspired task with those he would rely on to accomplish it. His words to them were clear and direct: "You see the trouble we are in.... Come, let us *build*" (verse 17, ESV). He emphasized God's initiative in all this: "I told them of the hand of my God which had been good upon me" (verse 18).

His call to action was immediately effective: "They said, 'Let us *rise up and build.*' Then they set their hands to *this good work*" (verse 18). Nehemiah went on to boldly express his faith in what they were setting out to do: "The God of heaven Himself will prosper us; therefore we His servants will *arise and build*" (verse 20).

With Nehemiah setting the example, "the people had a mind to *work*" (4:6), which is also the perfect mind-set for all our summer endeavors. In fact, the entire account of the wall's rebuilding (Nehemiah 1–6) serves as an invaluable guidebook on how to conduct summer undertakings.

We'll face obstacles and opposition to our efforts, and Nehemiah led the way in battling such opposition (2:19–20; 4:1–14; 6:1–14).

We'll experience weariness in our work, as the builders in Jerusalem did when they said, "The strength of the laborers is failing, and there is so much rubbish that we are not able to build the wall" (4:10). Nehemiah led the way in encouraging them onward, organizing them for their best efforts, and valiantly inspiring them when they faced attacks from their enemies (verses 13–23).

God's work cannot be accomplished apart from His enabling strength, help, and protection. It is therefore no surprise that Nehemiah led the way in clothing their work with prayer (verses 4–5, 9).

As Nehemiah did, we'll often need assistance from others, using their strengths and gifts. The book of Nehemiah emphasizes how the people pitched in to share all aspects of the work (3:1–32; 4:16–18).

We'll face distractions and frustrations caused by the shortcomings of others, and Nehemiah led the way in dealing firmly with such disappointments (5:1–13) and in maintaining his integrity throughout (verses 14–19).

For Nehemiah and the people of Judah, this particular "summer" of work would last only fifty-two days, until the wall was finished (6:15). It came about so quickly and in such a distinctive way that the neighboring peoples "perceived that this work was done by our God" (verse 16). When our summer labor follows the pattern set by Nehemiah and those he faithfully led, *God gets the glory!* Could anything better be said about our efforts?

As we follow Nehemiah's example in wise, diligent, prayerful work in our summers of opportunity, we will be able to say as he did, "The good hand of my God [was] upon me" (2:8). And we'll experience the genuine joy in our labor that God intends.

With your mind made sensitive to what summer labor is all about, I trust your eyes will be opened to recognize the helpful patterns and principles that we see throughout both Old and New Testaments, as men and women carry out their assignments and responsibilities in the face of inevitable challenges and obstacles. Think of Moses and the work God sent him back to Egypt to accomplish as well as his labor in a later season of leading Israel's redeemed people through the wilderness. Or consider Joshua and his monumental assignment of conquering Canaan, or Samuel's challenging undertaking to prepare the nation of Israel for a monarchy and then finding, anointing, and counseling the first two kings.

The list goes on and on, all the way to John's unique work in Revelation of receiving and committing to written form the visions given him by the Lord Jesus. The amazing variety of tasks pursued by the Lord's servants as recorded in Scripture represents an endless source of lessons and inspiration for our own summer labor.

Moving Forward from Spring to Summer

Spring is usually more popular than summer because it's often more pleasant to begin a new stage of life than to grow and mature in it. Weddings are fun; marriages are work. The first day of school can be exciting, but getting course assignments completed on time is a different story. Cuddling your cooing infant is exhilarating, but rearing that child for the next eighteen years requires sacrifice. Spring is about *beginnings;* summer is about *work.*

I've always found beginnings exhilarating, if not pleasant. I'm not saying I handled all my springs well—I've already related my numerous mishaps when starting kindergarten, high school, and university. Nonetheless, springs are exciting, in part, because we aren't sure if we "have what it takes" to succeed in our new stages of life.

I remember how I launched my modest basketball career. I was eleven years old and relatively tall for my age. My mother thought I would enjoy playing basketball in the local city league. Most of the kids on the team had already played for several years, while I didn't know the difference between a foul shot and a double dribble. I felt extremely inadequate. I was also more than a little annoyed with my mother for signing me up without asking my permission. In protest I adamantly refused to go to my first practice. In response to my pitiful defiance, my dear mother drew upon her extensive skills of persuasion, diplomacy, and rational argument: She grabbed a broom and chased me out of the house, uttering dire warnings if I didn't go! As apprehensive as I was of making a fool of myself on the basketball court, I was even more afraid of my mother because her threats were seldom hollow. I went reluctantly but subsequently developed a fondness for basketball that had a major positive effect on my life for years afterward.

Have you noticed there's a fine line between being scared to death and being excited? My two sons often informed me that they couldn't possibly become public speakers because they were too scared to talk in front of an audience. Yet this same pair of boys will fork over exorbitant amounts of money to bungee jump into deep canyons or will ride ridiculously scary roller coasters. It's ironic how people will avoid doing something perfectly safe because it frightens them and then turn around and readily do something dangerous so they can be afraid. It's like that with spring. Beginning new adventures can be daunting, but the corresponding excitement is what makes spring so seductive.

Once the initial thrill of a new stage wears off, we have to settle in to undertake the hard work that follows in summer. At times this transition from new beginnings into the labor that follows can be difficult.

When I was in college, people worried about me—a lot. My first months of university were fun and challenging, but as time rolled by, I spent more time hunting and playing hockey than studying and attending classes.

That habit came back to bite me a few years later. Over halfway through my final semester, I discovered that, due to a scheduling glitch, I wasn't officially enrolled in the sociology class that I'd been sporadically attending for several months. (Poignantly, it was a class on social deviancy.) This was my final semester, and I needed the class credits to graduate. The registrar assured me that correcting the problem was simple: since the class had fewer than twenty students, I needed only to secure my professor's signature on a form vouching that I'd been attending his class, and I would be officially enrolled. The problem was, I'd skipped so many classes that when I took the form to my teacher, he didn't recognize me.

Let's just say I didn't suffer from acute workaholism when I was in college.

But that all changed once I had a family and began my career. While I would not have won the Most Motivated Student award in my university years, I eagerly embraced the life stage of building my career and raising my family. I'll never forget signing the closing papers on our cute little starter home. We bought it at a time when interest rates were extremely high (a habit that has curiously stuck with me through several mortgages). The bank manager let us borrow the money we needed, for which we were greatly appreciative (until, of course, we entered the summer season of making mortgage payments at that interest rate). I was also on cloud nine when I began my role as pastor of my first congregation. Some of that euphoria dissipated in summer as some of my precious flock enlightened me through notes, calls, and occasional tantrums in my office about my numerous shortcomings.

And then there was the thrill of the birth of our children. Our oldest child was born two weeks prematurely. Both Lisa and I had worked all day, and I had played a softball game that evening. Just as we were wearily getting into bed that night, Lisa's water broke. Casting our exhaustion aside, we giddily packed Lisa's suitcase and drove to the hospital.

I'd faithfully attended the Lamaze classes, and I knew the drill. I would meticulously record the time of each contraction while comforting my sweetheart with loving and soothing words through the entire process.

After a long night with no progress, Lisa was given medication to make the contractions come faster. That's when the trouble started. The baby went into distress, and his heart rate dropped dangerously low. Suddenly hospital personnel burst into our room and raced my wife's gurney down the hallway. No one asked to see my carefully recorded twelve-hour labor log. Eight minutes later I was introduced to our firstborn son.

You would think that after the trauma of childbirth, the springtime of parenting wouldn't hold many fond memories. But of course that's not true. There's always something magical about beginnings.

Then came summer. During this season of productivity, I was advancing my career, partnering with my wife to rear our children, and paying off the mortgage and other bills necessary to keep our children's voracious appetites satisfied while maintaining clothes on their backs. Instead of my former sports car (at least, it had seemed like one to me), I now owned a minivan. Instead of living life on the edge, I was constantly implementing austerity programs and devising ways to get office work done even while on family vacations.

Ah yes, family vacations. Those were my Achilles heel. Now, I'm as willing to enjoy a holiday as the next guy, but being a task-oriented, Type A leader, I took my logistical responsibilities seriously. Everyone else's role was to have fun. My job was to get us where we needed to go—on time and under budget.

One year our family decided to drive from Alberta, Canada, to Disneyland in Southern California. That was two weeks in a minivan with three kids and a wife who wanted to stop for lunch before we cleared the city limits. Surely you feel my pain.

The night before we embarked on our epic journey, I carefully inspected the vehicle. Because I was always in the driver's seat, I normally never ventured back into the "cheap seats" of our van. However, before this marathon trip I wanted to ensure that everything was sparkling clean and in smooth working order. I was shocked to find moldy lumps of unrecognizable protoplasm (vaguely resembling tuna sandwiches), decomposing apple cores, rotting banana peels, sticky candy remnants, and Coke that had spilled into a cup holder and crystallized. And that was just where my wife sat!

I steeled myself and kept inspecting: toys and books, mittens and socks, long-lost homework pages, sports equipment, hair ribbons, and coins—on and on it went.

After clearing out the clutter, I used every funny-looking vacuum cleaner attachment we owned, plus gallons of industrial-strength cleaning sprays. When I was finished, that puppy was in pristine condition.

The next morning, at dawn's early light, the kids and I happily piled into our immaculate vessel. Not a dust particle to be found! I could see my reflection in the dash!

I carefully folded my map to the appropriate section (no GPS back then), reinforced its creases, and placed it comfortably within arm's reach. I clipped my newly polished sunglasses securely into the holder on the visor. I was partway through a speech to my children describing how well-organized and budget-friendly our trip was going to be when Lisa bustled out the door and began climbing into the vehicle.

Having missed her calling as a cruise ship entertainment director, she always tried to make our vacations as fun filled as possible. Realizing our kids had missed breakfast, my dear wife was carrying a stack of toast for distribution to the kids—*inside my spotless vehicle!*

"Stop right there!" I bellowed as I flung myself across the van to bar the door. "This is a crumb-free zone!"

To this day my family reminds me of how I insisted we all get out of the van and stand in the driveway to eat our toast. Then every passenger underwent a rigorous "crumb security check" before being granted reentry.

Oh yes, traveling with me on vacation was a blast.

I was keenly aware of the massive crater such vacations inflicted on our credit card. I dreaded gas stops because they always cost me far more than the tank of petrol. What should have been an efficient in-and-out pit stop at a roadside gas station became a prolonged snack run by my wife and kids. While I washed the windshield and checked the oil, they disappeared inside and returned chattering happily, laden with overpriced candies and soft drinks, oblivious to the fact that our van would morph into a landfill by the time we merged back onto the highway.

For me, the worst family vacation ordeal of all was the theme park. For starters, there's the price of admission. Egad! We didn't qualify for any discounts (believe me, I asked). So I calculated how much a day with Mickey was going to cost me *per hour,* then created an itinerary that would enable us to efficiently enjoy all the rides, see every show, and consume the cheapest food. It all came down to my master plan. You see, I don't *enjoy* theme parks; I *conquer* them!

At 0700 I bellowed into the darkness of our economy motel room: "All right, up and at 'em! We're burning daylight!" At 0900, our family was dutifully lined up in descending order for the wait at Disneyland's front gate. "Only half an hour now. Let's synchronize our watches! As soon as the gates open, pass everyone you can. We'll do a brisk march a hundred yards south down Main Street, then veer to the west fifty yards and fall in line for the Indiana Jones ride. I'll not tolerate any lollygagging! I heard the line for that ride can take two hours, so we want to knock that beast off first. Then we'll conduct a hard march to Fantasy Land, and…"

As my family trotted beside me from ride to ride, they would occasionally ask annoying questions like, "Dad, when are we going to stop at a bathroom?"

"Son," I would answer, "bathroom breaks are for the weak! Do you have any idea how many people will get in line ahead of you at the next ride while you waste precious time?"

We *did* conquer every ride and show. And in only a few weeks, I was back on speaking terms with my family.

I'm not sure what happened to me when I left my carefree spring season and entered summer as a parent, but there was no mistaking that a dramatic change had occurred.

The most prominent mental image of summer might well be a leisurely vacation at the beach. Summer, however, is primarily spent, not in leisure, but in work and growth. Will you be prepared to make the most of that season each time it comes your way? Or will you be like the man in the story Jesus told, the guy who started building a tower but came up short—to the amusement of mocking onlookers who said, "This man began to build and was not able to finish" (Luke 14:30).

To help us be ready to press forward in this crucial season, in the chapters to come, let's look at summer through the grid of four primary areas of life.

REFLECT AND RESPOND

1. What do you enjoy most about nature's season of summer? What do you like least about it?

2. Is summer your favorite season? Why or why not?

3. What single term would you generally use to describe the summers of your life? Successful? Laborious? Unproductive? Exhausting? Rewarding? Something else?

4. Whose life most inspires you? What insight can you gain by how that person spent his or her summer seasons?

5. To what extent do you see yourself as being designed by God for *labor*? What kind of labor do you feel most drawn to and best suited for?

6. If you're currently in a summer season, what do you project the harvest will be? What results are you anticipating?

12

SUMMER AND OUR IDENTITY

It's relatively easy to start something. We see people do this all the time as they enter a new spring. They typically appear excited, energetic, and confident, and it's easy to imagine their success. But if you want to really know people, observe how they conduct themselves in summer. Summer separates the boys from the men, the dreamers from the performers, the low-level employees from management.

Let me give you some examples.

One summer while I was in graduate school, I worked on a grounds-keeping crew in Texas, where one week the temperature hit 110 degrees. Nevertheless, because of my financial status, I was grateful for the employment, even in the heat.

One day I met Ben, a new hire. Ben was impressive. He was a body-builder who was going to try out later that summer for the offensive line of the football team at a major university. His biceps were the size of my waist. The guy looked like a Greek statue searching for a museum. He was always drinking superconcentrated vitamin and protein concoctions while nibbling on space-age, high-fiber snacks. He could spout off impressive statistics about body fat and muscle mass for hours. He made an extraordinary first impression.

The second impression, however, wasn't so good.

Once the introductions were over, the training complete, and Ben's push mower assigned, it didn't take long to realize something was wrong. The guy was lazy. He was also a bit of a baby. One day our crew was assigned to mow the grass on a property so extensive it included a landing strip. The grass went on forever, and much of it had to be cut with push mowers. It was one of those 110-degree days when Ben and I were lucky enough to land that coveted assignment.

Even at the best of times, Ben didn't exactly push himself. He would drone on about his optimum heart rate and cardiovascular something-or-other, all of which was beyond me. What I did know was that he was one slow worker. On this particular day he barely completed one lap before stopping under a tree to down a Gatorade. He eventually ventured out of the shade for one more cautious lap before lying down in the shade again and mumbling something about his electrolytes. I finished mowing the remainder of that massive field while he took a siesta.

And so the summer went.

You might be racking your brain wondering, *What NFL player or college great had the first name of Ben?* Well, don't waste your time. Ben's performance that summer revealed his character, and it wasn't conducive to football stardom.

Then there was Will. He felt called into Christian ministry, so he enrolled in a seminary and launched into a new stage of life. At first his decision to relocate with his wife to attend school seemed impressive. But as he entered the summer season of his graduate school years, his true colors began to show. Will was smart, in a lazy sort of way. His attitude was: "No church is going to ask to see a transcript of my grades. So why kill myself to earn an A when a C will suffice?"

Which reminds me of counsel I later received when I was a seminary president. I was told to treat my A students well, because some of them would one day become professors. I was advised to treat the B students graciously, because they would eventually become some of the best pastors in our denomination. But I was urged to take special care of my C students, because they would ultimately become seminary trustees!

But back to Will. When his classmates thoroughly reviewed their notes before the daily quiz, Will derided these "overachievers." Why endure unnecessary stress? As planned, Will left seminary as a C student. A church did call him. And, as he had smugly foretold, they never inquired about his school transcript. But as you might imagine, Will took his underperforming attitude into the ministry. Why be an A pastor, when a C pastor gets paid the same?

Not surprisingly, his congregation floundered. Eventually Will experienced an epiphany; he decided his talents lay not so much in the daily grind of the pastorate but in teaching others how to be ministers. Which reminds me of the adage "Those who can't, teach. And those who can't teach, teach gym."

Will called the local Bible college and alerted its academic dean to his immediate availability. To his dismay he discovered that to satisfy the standards of the accrediting agency, the school required its professors to hold a PhD. After receiving the same response from other institutions, Will decided he would have to return to school and pick up the required degree. That's when things got sticky. His application was declined because of—you guessed it—that C average.

Will never earned a doctorate and never became a professor. His behavior in summer prevented him from reaping the harvest he desired in autumn.

Summer is the season when one's character is both forged and revealed. At this point qualities such as perseverance, integrity, work ethic, and dependability are critical.

In our springtimes we all face many similar opportunities—to go to school, to get married, to become parents, to get new jobs. Everyone encounters such possibilities in life. But it's what we do with those opportunities in summer that sets people apart.

Some young couples are consumed with plans for a beautiful wedding ceremony and the honeymoon that follows. They spare no expense on their fairy tale extravaganza but later put inadequate effort into sustaining a successful marriage. Others may desperately want to have a baby, yet they show themselves unwilling to make the necessary sacrifices required of good parents. Job candidates may come up with strong résumés and make a great impression in an interview, while their track record in previous jobs leaves much to be desired.

Spring is when we get our foot in the door; summer is what we do once we're inside.

Notice what the book of Proverbs says about this:

He who has a slack hand becomes poor,
But the hand of the diligent makes rich.
He who gathers in summer is a wise son;
He who sleeps in harvest is a son who causes shame. (10:4–5)

The lazy man does not roast what he took in hunting,
But diligence is man's precious possession. (12:27)

The soul of a lazy man desires, and has nothing;
But the soul of the diligent shall be made rich. (13:4)

The wise woman builds her house,
But the foolish pulls it down with her hands. (14:1)

In my experience, hiring people has provided certain challenges. An interviewer must peer beyond the outward appearance and the glowing résumé to discern the candidate's character—to see if there's a reflection of the kind of qualities those Proverbs passages speak of. And it isn't easy.

I remember hearing about a manager of an engineering firm who was trying to fill a vacancy. He was far too busy to weed through the dozens of identical-looking résumés that had accumulated on his desk. When his assistant urged him to examine the stack of résumés, the preoccupied manager took the top half of the pile and casually dropped it into the garbage can. Then in all seriousness he explained to his colleague, "Those people aren't lucky. Our firm doesn't need unlucky people working for it." (I don't recommend this approach!)

Whether it's the summer of their college years, their careers, or their parenthood, those who strive for excellence, persevere in adversity, continue learning, and demonstrate integrity in all they do will amass an enviable track record. Such people can genuinely look forward to the time of harvest.

Summer is truly a make-or-break season in defining and determining who we really are.

REFLECT AND RESPOND

1. In what ways can the toil of summer help you discover your identity?

2. How has your sense of identity changed in the summers you've experienced in earlier stages of life?

3. What are the most significant ways in which your character has been shaped by your previous seasons of hard work?

4. How would you describe your work ethic in general? Do you see yourself as a hard worker? Do others see you this way?

5. Whatever season you're in, what is one particular assumption about yourself that it would be wise to examine and reconsider at this time in your life?

13

Our Relationships
in Summer

Some relationships are lifelong, such as those with a spouse and children. Others are more seasonal, such as associations with colleagues at work or friends from church. Let's explore what we should expect from these relationships during our summer seasons.

Marriage

As couples begin their marriage, they typically discover the need for adjustments as they learn to live with each other. Leaving the toilet seat down, keeping your side of the bathroom sink orderly, and chewing with your mouth closed can be quickly dealt with if both parties are willing. But once a baby arrives, the adjustments required for continued marital harmony can seem monumental. This transition into a new stage of marriage creates enormous stress.

Every time a couple enters a new stage of married life, they must reinvent their marriage. For example, newlyweds can enjoy their relationship without the distraction, added responsibility, and expense of children. However, once children arrive, couples must make alterations to their relationship if they are to continue to thrive. Eventually the empty nest stage of marriage will come. Tragically, many couples divorce near this stage because they fail to invest the summertime labor required for reconstructing their relationship after their children leave home.

Retirement years also bring unique challenges to marriage. One CEO friend of mine used to run a large corporation. After he retired, he established an office in his home. On the first day of retirement, he barked out an order to his wife the way he used to at work—and was quickly made aware that he was *not* the CEO at home!

The problem with some marriages is that they remain static. Life changes, but couples fail to properly develop and adjust their relationship throughout the changing seasons.

I enjoy weddings, and I've officiated at several. They're always beautiful. Family and friends come from near and far to share in the couple's elation. The bride is always glowing. The groom usually looks a little bewildered. Together the lovebirds state their vows and emphatically declare their boundless love for their soul mate. The anticipation, the love, and the romance are genuine. But after the wedding is over, the gifts are opened, and the honeymoon concludes, the marriage begins. Summer comes.

My honeymoon didn't get off to an impressive start. Because we were impoverished college students, my dear mother-in-law helped us find a great "deal" on a cozy cottage at a lake. The day after our wedding, we vacated our luxurious bridal suite at a posh hotel and drove six hours to our little love nest in the woods. One look at the isolated, rustic, one-room clapboard cabin and we knew why it had been available at such late notice! I carried my sweetheart across the threshold, and after a sweeping perusal of our accommodations, she crumpled onto the bed in a fit of tears. My wife has never done rustic very well. We lasted a day and a half before we packed up and went to stay with my in-laws.

Marriage looks different from the outside than from the inside. You've probably known a few disenchanted young brides who dreamed of their lovely wedding and planned every detail. The big day was perfect in every way; but afterward their marriage was a disaster. I know one beautiful young bride who returned from her honeymoon and immediately filed for divorce! While most young couples fantasize about wedded bliss in spring, couples in summer must roll up their sleeves and engage in the gritty business of building a marriage.

Why do Hollywood celebrities gush and enthuse about their latest "main squeeze" one month, then conduct tell-all interviews after their split the next? Typically they buy into the myth that a relationship exists in a perpetual springtime. Other couples simply aren't willing to make the effort. I know a man whose wife asked him when their children were young if they could go for marital counseling. She was hoping they could breathe fresh life into their relationship. The husband agreed there were problems, but he balked at the counselor's high hourly rate and decided they didn't need professional help. Today they're divorced.

Over the years I've watched a phenomenon in churches. If you offer a course on marriage, guess who typically signs up? The couples with the healthiest marriages! And who's invariably too disinterested or too busy or too broke to attend? You guessed it. The couples who need it most. Why? People who are committed to working on their relationships are prepared to make the necessary investment.

My wife once had an awkward phone call with someone who had committed adultery. "Lisa," the woman told her, "you're lucky. You have a good marriage." The woman missed the point. Couples don't luck into good marriages like winning a door prize at a school carnival. Spouses build strong marriages by working hard during summer.

I remember the first marriage enrichment seminar Lisa and I attended. The theme was communication. We learned that if couples would simply interact honestly, openly, and lovingly, there would no longer be any reason for arguments or bickering.

At the conclusion of the retreat, we all looked into our spouse's eyes and committed ourselves not to fight or argue anymore but to faithfully apply our new communication tools. Then we headed home.

Some friends of ours had been at the retreat with us, and when it concluded, they suggested we all reunite that evening and go out for a hamburger. We were game.

But after Lisa and I arrived home, the stress of the retreat and the lack of sleep in the primitive setting proved too much for us, and we had an argument. We hadn't even lasted the weekend! We were somewhat consoled when our friends arrived late for hamburgers and sheepishly confessed they had argued all the way home.

I'm not saying that knock-down-drag-out fights are the way to go, but neither should we kid ourselves. There's no easy road or shortcut to strong marriages.

CHILDREN

Bringing up children isn't for the fainthearted, the selfish, or the lazy. Conceiving children is the easy part. Rearing them can be loads of fun at times, but it's definitely not easy. In each new stage in the lives of their children, parents need to adjust the way they relate to them. Summer seasons are the times to make those adjustments.

For example, consider my middle child, Daniel. I could easily relate to him when he was a preschooler. He was a pudgy-faced, gentle child with loads of personality. He had a stubborn streak and a disdain for naps, but overall he was easy to care for.

The year I assumed the presidency of a small seminary in Canada initiated a brand-new season in our family's life. I enthusiastically tackled my new job, arriving at the office before daylight each morning and addressing every issue with a can-do spirit. Meanwhile our two sons enrolled in a new school. I've already recounted Daniel's aversion to show and tell. That was only the beginning. One day my wife called my office, distraught. Six-year-old Daniel had decided he much preferred being at home with his little sister playing video games than wasting his precious time at school. So at recess he made a break for it, traversing busy streets and back alleys until he arrived home to his beloved Nintendo. Thus began Daniel's jailbreak stage of life.

How does a father relate to a six-year-old who heads his elementary school's Most Wanted list? This wasn't exactly the kind of challenge I'd been tackling with my executive team.

After a few "escapes from Alcatraz," Daniel's long-suffering teacher decided to keep him in the classroom during recess to dissuade him from making another break. *Child's play,* thought our little Houdini, who took flight while his teacher's back was turned. At home he tiptoed in the back door, and his mother found him in the den moments later playing Mario Kart just as the phone rang. That boy had a remarkable homing instinct!

I tried reasoning with Daniel, explaining the dangers of crossing busy streets and detailing the angst it put school officials through whenever they discovered a child was AWOL. I even attempted flagrant bribery and an escalating reward system, all to no effect.

Finally I put my foot down and explained that he *would not* come home anymore and that if he did, dire consequences would ensue. He *did* come home, dire consequences ensued, and Daniel never broke out of school again. I'd been forced to adopt a heavy-handed relationship with my son. At that point it was truly a matter of life or death, and since he was too young to understand how dangerous his actions were, I laid down the law.

If Daniel's heart is into something, there's no stopping him. If his heart is *not* into something—well, let's just say we've had some long conversations.

Fast-forward to Daniel in middle school. He was going through a difficult period of being unable to sleep at night. He was also struggling with some stressful relationships at school. He finally reached a low point where he couldn't take it anymore, so he holed up in his bedroom and refused to go back to school.

I'm ashamed to confess that my uppermost reaction at the time was one of impatience with the interruption. In those days I was extremely busy with a demanding job that involved extensive travel. The last thing I needed was for my teenage son to refuse to attend school. So I pulled out the same tools that had worked for me six years earlier and began uttering unspeakable threats of what I'd do to him if he didn't shape up and go to school.

This time, however, I hit a brick wall. My son was a teenager now. The issues he was facing were more complex and painful than merely missing his little sister and Nintendo. Daniel was hurting and feeling overwhelmed. Having his dad harp at him to suck it up and be a man only made matters worse.

I clearly remember that tense evening. Looking back, I desperately wish I could retrieve the unkind words I hurled at my son that day. I'd been thinking only about myself. I wanted a simple solution so I could get back to my own problems.

In that moment I came to a realization: I either had to alter my relationship with my son, or I was going to lose whatever relationship I still had.

Daniel is a "feeler," while I'm a cognitive-oriented person. When Daniel became emotional, he appeared to me to be entirely irrational. Since I am a decisive decision maker and problem solver, it went against all my instincts not to identify and implement the most basic, cost-effective solution to the problem. But a simple remedy wasn't what Daniel needed.

Ultimately we chose to educate him at home. My wife and I had never considered homeschooling our kids before, even though Lisa is a trained secondary school teacher. The path we chose wasn't easy. Lisa suddenly had the responsibility of ensuring Daniel earned all the credits required to eventually enter university. (Our other two children, meanwhile, were in separate public schools—on opposite ends of town.) I taught Daniel social studies and also tried to connect with him so he knew I was on his side and believed in him.

It was a lot of work. But it proved to be one of the best decisions we ever made.

Now revisit Daniel as an eighteen-year-old. He'd been homeschooled through some extremely turbulent teenage years. He'd suffered a major, untreatable sleep disorder. Thankfully, due in large part to his long-suffering mother, Daniel was going to graduate from high school on schedule. But what next? His older brother had marched off directly to college. Daniel needed to find his own unique identity and career path. When he was six, I had insisted he go to school. When he was thirteen, I still insisted he be schooled, but we adapted so he could do it at home. But at eighteen? Could I insist on *anything*?

Daniel was an adult, albeit one who wasn't sure he wanted the accompanying responsibilities. The years of insomnia had taken their toll. He'd thrown himself into the church youth group, playing in some bands and sports, but he couldn't face the thought of university and its rigorous demands or even a full-time job. He was unsure what his future held. His high school stage was coming to a close, but his next stage of life appeared daunting. I knew I couldn't treat him like a six-year-old or a thirteen-year-old; I had to adapt my relationship with my son once again.

Lisa and I both recognized that sending Daniel to college at that point would be a waste of his time and our money. Allowing him to lounge around the house every day would lead to conflicts the magnitude of which had not been witnessed since the battle at Helm's Deep in Lord of the Rings. As parents we knew that Daniel had plenty of gray matter to succeed academically, but without a vision for his future, he would lack the motivation to make the required effort. With Daniel it has always come down to motivation. Merely insisting he get a job and flip burgers for the next year wouldn't speak to Daniel's soul or solve his need for direction in life. So the three of us—Lisa, Daniel, and I—concocted a plan. We decided he would leave the country, alone, at age eighteen.

Since my job requires frequent travel, I accrue numerous frequent-flier miles. Another perk of my profession is that through the years I've met many remarkable people around the world. So I arranged for Daniel to spend a year volunteering his services to various worthy causes. After high school he went to Botswana, South Africa, Greece, Brazil, Norway, and Germany. He volunteered in refugee camps in Athens. He spent time with college students in Botswana and even entered their dance competition. (He didn't advance past warmups.) He traveled to impoverished villages along the Amazon River, entertaining ragamuffin children with his guitar while medical volunteers treated patients. He worked with teenagers in a church in Norway. He heard amazing stories from people who knew life's value and potential. He discovered that the world is much larger than the small town where he grew up. He also experienced the satisfaction of making a positive difference in the lives of others.

Throughout his sojourn I e-mailed Daniel, trying to coach and encourage him. At the end of that year, I asked him if he'd heard God's voice during his odyssey. He most definitely had. He'd experienced firsthand what God could do through his life. Daniel was determined never to settle for anything less.

Seven years have passed since then. Daniel completed college and now is in seminary working on a master's degree in preparation for a life of Christian ministry. He has been intimately involved in starting two church plants, one in South Carolina and another in San Francisco. He's working two part-time jobs and recently coauthored his first book with his older brother, Mike.[18] He has spoken before audiences of thousands and has even met with the president of the Philippines. He married his soul mate and no longer struggles with his health. He signed a contract with a publisher to write a fantasy trilogy titled *The Lost City Chronicles*.

And as you've probably guessed, now that he's married, I've had to rework our relationship yet again!

I'm not relating Daniel's accomplishments to boast about my parenting skills or any unique insights into the developmental stages of children. I've made numerous parental mistakes, and I have a bucketload of regrets. I also realize that not everyone has the air miles to send a struggling child overseas. But the point is this: as your children enter each new stage of their lives, you must make the adjustments necessary to continue enjoying a thriving and close relationship with them.

FRIENDS

Social media sites such as Facebook have become wildly popular in connecting people around the world. But one lamentable side effect is that the definition of *friend* has changed. In social media terminology, a friend is anyone who agrees to accept your friend request. All people have to do is click the Accept button, and, voilà, you've become virtual friends. Social media and public forums are here to stay, which means it's more important than ever to be discerning about the many levels of friendship.

Spring is typically when we make new friends; summer is when those relationships mature.

Notice some of what Scripture says about true friends:

A friend loves at all times. (Proverbs 17:17)

There is a friend who sticks closer than a brother. (Proverbs 18:24)

Two are better than one,
Because they have a good reward for their labor.
For if they fall, one will lift up his companion.
But woe to him who is alone when he falls,
For he has no one to help him up.
Again, if two lie down together, they will keep warm;
But how can one be warm alone?
Though one may be overpowered by another, two can
    withstand him.
And a threefold cord is not quickly broken. (Ecclesiastes 4:9–12)

The sagacious author of Ecclesiastes asserted that if we're going to enjoy life and find success, we must experience it *with others*. As we enter each new stage of life, we may make new friends along the way, but once we meet our new college roommate or a colleague at work or a fellow church member, the quality and depth of that relationship rests largely in our hands.

When I took my first job as a senior pastor, I faced a tough assignment. My church had suffered seven years of dramatic decline and endured numerous problems on multiple levels. I attended a meeting of ministers and met other pastors from my denomination. They all seemed like great guys who could teach me a lot. I approached one of them who was about my age and asked if he was interested in meeting regularly to support each other. I sensed he needed some encouragement, and I knew I could learn a lot from him. He wasn't interested! I kept looking.

Later I approached Mike, the pastor of an inner-city ministry focused on reaching the down-and-out. It seemed an unlikely match. Mike's church consisted mostly of poor people with addictions; I led a typical suburban church. We began meeting every week, and a great friendship developed that sustained both of us over the ensuing years.

I also became friends with Bob. He was the longest tenured minister in our pastors' group, led the largest church, and was a busy man. Whenever I faced a challenge or problem beyond my limited expertise, I scheduled lunch with Bob (there was a great Chinese buffet near his church), and he would graciously walk me through the issue.

The friendships I developed with my fellow pastors enriched my life and strengthened my ministry. Likewise, I did all I could to encourage them. I learned that whether you lead a large organization or a small one, you need friends. The quality of friendships depends on how hard you work at your relationships in summer.

Some people have numerous relationships; others have only a few. Yet what is important is not necessarily the number of people we relate to but the quality of our interactions with them. Spring is when we become acquainted with others; summer is when we work to really know, bless, and enjoy them. The quality of the relationships you enjoy today is a direct reflection of how hard you worked on them in summer.

REFLECT AND RESPOND

1. Have your relationships with your spouse, children, or friends matured during summer? How?

2. Consider your relationships with your family, friends, and colleagues. How would you like to see these relationships improve? What might you do to ensure they do?

3. Do you have any relationships you've neglected or been lazy with? If so, how could you breathe new life into them?

4. Do you have any broken relationships? If so, are you prepared to ask for forgiveness? Are you willing to do what it takes to mend them?

5. Do you know people close to you who are currently in a summer season? How could you encourage them with something you've learned so far from this book?

14

Our Roles in Summer

As we saw earlier, spring is the time to embrace new roles at school, at work, at church, at home, or in our communities. Summer, meanwhile, is when we get our hands dirty. This is of course what separates mere officeholders from people who experience great success. "The price of greatness," Winston Churchill observed, "is responsibility."

There's a modern misconception that those who are successful in life or in business or in their family are merely lucky. But there's much more to it than that.

I love biographies. I have shelves full of them in my home. I read about presidents, business leaders, generals, kings, queens, prime ministers, and leaders from every field. I read Winston Churchill's classic twenty-three-hundred-page biography on his ancestor, the Duke of Marlborough, while vacationing in Hawaii with my family (which positions me on my kids' boring scale somewhere between watching paint dry and the color beige). But you know what I've found? While successful leaders exhibit a wide diversity in character and worldviews (try reading biographies of Julius Caesar and Steve Jobs back to back), the one thing successful leaders have in common is this: *they aren't lazy!*

Of course some of them went overboard in their labors. John Rockefeller went to work the morning of his wedding! He also became the wealthiest tycoon of his day. Most of these people weren't merely focused on earning money. They were passionate about what they were doing. They invested themselves completely in their roles during summer.

In his book *Tribes,* Seth Godin points out that some people endure an entire year at their jobs just to enjoy their two-week vacation. Godin offers this challenge: "Instead of wondering when your next vacation is, maybe you ought to set up a life you don't need to escape from."[19]

John Wooden was the UCLA basketball coach who won an unprecedented ten national championships and whose career included a period in which he won an astounding thirty-eight tournament games in a row. On July 29, 2009, *Sporting News Magazine* voted Wooden number one on their list of the top fifty coaches of all time. Generally, when we think of people like him, we remember their stellar achievements at the peak of their careers. Yet Wooden experienced a long, dry summer of hard work before he achieved the autumn of success. Wooden coached at UCLA for fifteen years before he won his first national championship. Throughout the summer season of his coaching career, he continually honed his skills until his teams became unbeatable.

Tom Landry is known for coaching the Dallas Cowboys for twenty-nine seasons and winning two Super Bowls and numerous honors over that period. However, he went 0-11-1 in his first season as head coach and won five or fewer games in each of his first five seasons.

Like Wooden and Landry, many achievers who eventually became legends began their careers inauspiciously. They ultimately made enormous contributions in their fields, but it took their summer years to master their skills for the success they would experience later on.

The 2010 movie *The King's Speech* won dozens of international awards from the motion picture industry and from film critic groups. The movie recounts the story of King George VI. Known in his younger days by his first name, Albert (Bertie for short), he wasn't supposed to become king because his older brother, Edward, was first in line to succeed their father, George V. Moreover, Edward was far more talented and "kingly" than Albert, who had a pronounced stammer, suffered chronic stomach problems, and was knock-kneed, easily moved to tears, and left handed at a time when southpaws were viewed as having a disability.

Nevertheless, Albert dutifully worked hard to fulfill his royal duties as a prince. He joined the navy and fought in World War I. After stammering through several disastrous public speeches, he enlisted a speech coach named Lionel Logue. When his older brother Edward gave up the throne in order to wed an American divorcée, Albert reluctantly ascended the throne as George VI at age forty-one. His decades of labor in summer had prepared him for what would be the greatest role of his life.

Those who work hardest and smartest in summer are the most likely to enjoy a glorious harvest in autumn. It's that simple.

REFLECT AND RESPOND

1. Of all your most important roles in your life, in which ones, if any, are you now experiencing a summer season, requiring extensive labor?

2. Looking back on your past, in what ways have your roles developed in the summer seasons you've known, the times of your hardest work?

3. How much do you welcome responsibility? Do you see yourself as having a large capacity for responsibilities?

4. What are the most valuable skills that are required for your life's roles at this time? How can you further develop those skills?

5. Have you ever grown weary of your work during a summer
   season? If so, how do you motivate yourself to stick with it
   until your work is done? If you've ever quit certain roles
   before the finish line, how has that cost you?

15

SUMMER AND OUR FAITH

While spring is when God invites us to enter into a deeper, more vibrant walk with Him, summer is when we put in the time it takes to get there.

One of Jesus's most famous parables is about a sower (Matthew 13:3–9). A farmer went out and scattered seed on his field. Some seed fell on shallow ground. The spring season was great! The seeds germinated, and plants began growing. But because the soil was so poor, the summer sun quickly scorched the plants.

Other seed landed amid thorns. Again spring appeared promising. The seeds germinated, and plants began growing. But over the course of summer, the thorns choked out the plants, and they were lost.

Seed also fell on good soil. In spring those seeds took root, and plants began growing. But in this case, as the summer sun shone brightly, the plants thrived and ultimately bore a bountiful harvest.

Each plant was birthed in spring. However, it was summer that determined what the harvest produced in autumn.

I've watched numerous scenarios of this parable play out. The Word of God can be sown into people's lives all across the auditorium during a worship service. Everyone in the congregation hears the same truth and has the identical opportunity to respond. However, once the euphoria of spring has passed and the hard work of summer sets in, the results vary widely.

I've had many sincere people tell me over the years what they sensed God wanted to do in their lives. They had faithfully followed through with what God told them, and the results were astounding. Others allowed the blistering summer heat to parch the divine sapling in their souls, and eventually the fresh work God had initiated in their lives withered on the vine.

It's not always easy to follow through on commitments. The challenge of summer, of course, is that it's often the busiest season of life. Whether we're students or parents or employees, summer is when we have to "get 'er done," as a friend of mine likes to say. It can therefore seem inconvenient and distracting to focus on matters of faith when we have so much schoolwork, business travel, or shuttling of children to do.

Yet often it's not in the prayer closet but in the midst of the busyness of life that God reveals some of His greatest insights. Elisha was plowing his field when Elijah passed by and invited him to become a prophet of God (1 Kings 19:19–21). Matthew was working at his tax collection booth when Jesus offered him the invitation of a lifetime (Luke 5:27–28). If these people had waited until things slowed down before they took time for God, they would have missed the most amazing moments of their spiritual journeys.

A DIVINE WORK AND A GATED COMMUNITY

I've come to greatly appreciate Burl Cain, the warden at Louisiana State Penitentiary in Angola, outside of Baton Rouge, and locally called Angola Prison.[20] When Cain became the warden, Angola was one of the largest and most violent maximum security prisons in America. Bloodshed was commonplace. Inmates slept in shifts to protect one another from being harmed during the night.

More than thirty-seven hundred of the fifty-two hundred inmates were serving life sentences. The average incarceration for those not serving life was around ninety years. Each year Cain buried more inmates than he released through the front gate.

During Cain's first year, he was asked to oversee the execution of an inmate. When everything was ready, Cain gave the thumbs-down signal, and the man was soon dead. That night, troubled by how casually he'd ushered another human being into eternity, Cain realized he had no idea if the man had ever heard the gospel of Jesus Christ. Due to the pressure of running the massive complex, Cain had never considered that God might want to work powerfully through his life while he was in the midst of the most challenging role of his career.

Cain decided to make the study course *Experiencing God* available to the residents on death row. Eventually the study was offered throughout the entire prison. Numerous prisoners had life-transforming encounters with God as a result. Acts of violence dropped by 73 percent.

My father and my brother Tom and I have spoken with the men imprisoned there. One inmate told me that Angola, once known as America's most violent prison, is now referred to as "Louisiana's largest gated community"!

Many of the men who studied *Experiencing God* felt God calling them into Christian ministry. New Orleans Baptist Theological Seminary eventually opened a Bible college inside the prison to train inmates to be ministers. I had the privilege of teaching one of those seminary classes. The room was filled with more than sixty prison-garbed fellows of all ages, attentively taking notes. It was unlike any class I'd ever taught before.

The changes in the prison were so dramatic that wardens from other prisons asked Cain for his secret. Angola began sending "missionaries" to other penitentiaries. Those who had taken *Experiencing God* and who had graduated from the Bible college were sent out in pairs to other prisons where they could start churches and share the same hope they'd found at Angola.

As I sat eating dinner with Burl Cain one evening, he recounted with amazement what God had done. A humble man, he had simply been trying to do the best job he could in the face of enormous challenges. But he discovered that right in the middle of the biggest responsibility of his life, God intended to do a miracle.

Summer's Yield

So we've seen the big truth about summer: it's a time for work. And no one else can do it for us.

Those who understand this fact and invest the required effort will grow, mature, and experience success. Those who choose instead to take it easy in summer will never experience life abundantly as God intended.

Summers may seem long, hot, and exhausting, but eventually they can lead to an amazing harvest. Autumn's abundant yield is the culmination of spring and summer. In the chapters to come, we'll look at why planting in spring and working hard in summer is so worth the effort.

Reflect and Respond

1. In what ways has your faith grown throughout each summer stage of your life, the times of your hardest work?

2. If your Christian life is the result of choices you've made, do you need to make any adjustments in how you're presently walking with God? Of all your life's endeavors, how high in priority has your walk with God been? Is it one of the first responsibilities to be neglected when you get busy or distracted? If so, how has that affected your Christian life?

3. How has God developed the quality of endurance in your life and faith? What need for further growth in this quality do you detect in your life?

4. What particular responsibilities require the most commitment from you at this time in your life? What can you do to strengthen your commitment in these critical areas?

5. Has God sown words of promise into your life that have not yet become a reality? Reflect on what God said to you previously and on how carefully you followed through with it. Are you missing out on something God intended to do in your life?

16

AUTUMN: HARVEST TIME

Confession time: I like cemeteries. My children think that's creepy. But isn't it intriguing how an epitaph on a tombstone can encapsulate an entire life, though it's usually not even a complete sentence?

Over the years some unusual inscriptions have been carved onto tombstones. For example, consider that of Lester Moore, a Wells Fargo agent who was shot and killed during an attempted holdup. His resting place reads: "Here lies Lester Moore. Four slugs from a .44. No Les. No Moore."

Then there's George Johnson, who inadvertently purchased a stolen horse, then blithely rode it into town, where he was immediately arrested and hung as a horse thief despite his vehement protests. His tombstone reads: "Hanged by mistake, he was right, we was wrong. But we hung him up, and now he's gone."

You can find a tombstone in Fort Wallace, Kansas, that says, "He tried to make two jacks beat a pair of aces."

In Ruidoso, New Mexico, a headstone reads: "Here lies John Yeast. Pardon me for not rising."

John Strange, a British attorney, has this commemoration: "Here lies an honest lawyer, and that is Strange."

In Lee County, Mississippi, a grave marker sports this succinct, if unrefined, summation: "Once I wasn't, then I was, now I ain't again."

An overworked housewife apparently wrote her own inscription, which says: "Everything here is exact to my wishes; because no one eats, there is no washing dishes."

There was a cook who burned to death after she fell asleep working over a hot woodstove. Her loved ones memorialized her with the rather tactless epitaph, "Well done, good and faithful servant."

There's also this indignant message: "I *told* you I was sick."

I also love the following ones translated from Spanish:

"Gustava Gumersinda Gutierrez Guzman 1934–1989: Rest in peace. A memory from all your sons (except Ricardo, who did not pay any money)."

"Here is resting my dearest wife, Brunjilda Jalamonte 1973–1997: Lord, please welcome her with the same joy I send her to you."

"Here rests Pancrazio Juvenales 1968–1993: He was a good husband, a wonderful father, but a bad electrician."

When people were asked what they would like to have on their tombstones, the suggestions offered included these:

"Pardon my dust."

"Well…that's that then."

"I saw this coming."

"Now I lay me down to sleep; the room is cramped, but the rent's dirt cheap."

It's a topic that people like to joke about—this side of the grave, anyway. On the other hand, countless final resting places are marked in all seriousness by inscriptions that seek to capture the essence of what was truly accomplished in the lives of the people buried there and what was most appreciated about them by their friends, loved ones, and acquaintances.

As we move into discussing the autumns of life, we're focusing on the season that typically provides the most content for the memorials, epitaphs, and eulogies that will follow later on.

Life's autumn seasons are generally when people make their greatest contributions. They gather the seeds they planted in spring and labored over during summer to produce a harvest in fall. As Ecclesiastes 3 notes, there is "a time to plant, and a time to pluck what is planted" (verse 2). Autumn is plucking season.

Every stage of life has four seasons, and autumn marks the peak of each stage and the climax of everything that has gone before. This is the season when people draw upon their strengths, successes, failures, and the wisdom gained along the way. As a result, autumn is generally the most productive and rewarding of the seasons.

The Picture for Us in Nature

Autumn has always been my favorite season, partly because the sweltering heat of summer has dissipated while the gray coldness of winter looms on the horizon. In the fall the air grows crisp. As morning dawns, the ground may be whitewashed with frost as the sultry summer nights are whisked aside by temperatures dipping increasingly lower after dusk. Nature displays a peculiar sense of urgency during fall as animals and birds instinctively prepare for the imminent cold and harshness that relentlessly approach.

The foliage of autumn is breathtaking. Deciduous trees transform into colorful masterpieces of bright oranges, reds, and yellows. Leaves that were lush and green during summer now morph overnight into fiery colors. Then they grudgingly release their grip on the branches and flutter to the ground, creating a brilliantly colored carpet that's often whipped into a fiery flurry by autumn's brisk winds. Flowers that paraded their beauty throughout summer now begin to wilt and fade. As their vitality ebbs away, the petals shrivel and return to the earth.

Vast grain fields sway in the breeze like an endless golden ocean. In the harvest the grain stalks that rose majestically into the sky are plucked clean, stripped and shorn, then plowed back into the earth.

Orchards, which only recently had been laden with fruit, now lie pillaged and abandoned. Fruit stands pop up along the roadside, laden with luscious delights of another harvest.

The sky hosts parades of migratory fowl, retreating in ranks from the approaching bleakness while abandoning human captives to their fate. Squirrels and birds energetically collect food to store in preparation for the uncertain season ahead. Whereas spring eagerly anticipated the coming summer in hopes of bounty, autumn peers ahead to winter with prayers that it won't be overly harsh.

Autumn dramatically affects people's lives. Farmers rise before dawn and work until late into the night, gathering grain into silos before sleet and snow strike. There's a palpable sense of relief when all the harvest has finally been gathered for another year.

Meanwhile, children return to school in droves after their summer reprieve. Football begins in earnest, entertaining crowds of enthusiastic fans. Baseball season draws to its annual classic finish, while hockey teams commence their marathon for Lord Stanley's cup.

Like every other season, autumn is filled with a mixture of anticipation as well as anxiety. Families gather to celebrate the harvest and to recall the year's blessings. But autumn isn't without its more sobering aspects. It reminds us of nature's inexorable end. Farmers live in trepidation of early snows or bitter frosts. This is hurricane season; enormous storms with innocuous, alphabetical names thrash the coastlands.

There's a sense of urgency in autumn. Time grows short. The prospect of a glorious harvest is at hand, but so also are darkening storms.

THE PICTURE FOR US IN SCRIPTURE

The Bible chronicles a wide variety of characters traversing through autumn.

Deborah's wisdom and sound judgment as God's spokesperson became so famous that eventually people came from all over the region to obtain her counsel (Judges 4:5). Even the army's top general refused to march into battle unless she accompanied his troops (verse 8).

Elijah was in his autumn season as a prophet when he dramatically called down fire from heaven on Mount Carmel (1 Kings 18). When the grizzled mouthpiece of God delivered his divine message, an entire nation ground to a halt. Elijah subsequently anointed the kings of the future as well as his own powerful successor (19:15–16).

Hezekiah was in his fall season as king when he bravely withstood the threats of the Assyrian warmonger, Sennacherib. Every other nation had crumbled like soda crackers before the Assyrian potentate, but Hezekiah beat the odds and outlived his nemesis (2 Kings 19).

John the Baptist reached the pinnacle of his ministry when large crowds came to hear him preach at the Jordan River and when he ultimately baptized the long-awaited Messiah (Matthew 3:5–6, 13–17). This was John's autumn zenith as he lived out his divine calling to be a voice crying in the wilderness, preparing the way for the Lord.

The preeminent autumn theme in Scripture is that of *fruitfulness*. The Bible insists that our lives are meant to be productive spiritually and in many other ways as well.

Paul writes "that we should bear fruit to God" (Romans 7:4). He prays for believers to be "filled with the fruits of righteousness which are by Jesus Christ, to the glory and praise of God" (Philippians 1:11); he prays for believers to "walk worthy of the Lord, fully pleasing Him, being fruitful in every good work and increasing in the knowledge of God" (Colossians 1:10).

Paul's words hearken back to God's original calling for us, when He first created man and woman: "Then God blessed them, and God said to them, 'Be fruitful'" (Genesis 1:28).

That calling to fruitfulness receives new impetus in the words of Christ on the night before His death on the cross. Speaking to His disciples, He fixed in their minds the image of the vine and its branches and used it to emphasize the priority of fruitfulness and to teach them its most profound principles:

> I am the true vine, and My Father is the vinedresser. Every branch in Me that does not *bear fruit* He takes away; and every branch that *bears fruit* He prunes, that it may *bear more fruit*.... Abide in Me, and I in you. As the branch cannot *bear fruit* of itself, unless it abides in the vine, neither can you, unless you abide in Me.
>
> I am the vine, you are the branches. He who abides in Me, and I in him, *bears much fruit;* for without Me you can do nothing. If anyone does not abide in Me, he is cast out as a branch and is withered; and they gather them and throw them into the fire, and they are burned. If you abide in Me, and My words abide in you, you will ask what you desire, and it shall be done for you. By this My Father is glorified, *that you bear much fruit;* so you will be My disciples. (John 15:1–8)

This fruitfulness that Jesus speaks of isn't instantaneous but follows the sowing of springtime and the labor of summer. And it's well worth waiting for. Scripture often speaks of "the joy of harvest" (Isaiah 9:3), when even "those who sow in tears shall reap in joy" (Psalm 126:5). This is a deeply satisfying joy, a rewarding fulfillment that our Creator designed us to experience. Springtime may have its thrills and summer its pleasures, but they hardly compare with autumn's harvest joy.

In that John 15 passage about the fruitful branches of the vine, Jesus goes on to tell His disciples, "These things I have spoken to you, that My *joy* may remain in you, and that your *joy* may be *full*" (verse 11). Our deepest experience of autumn in our lives truly brings a "joy inexpressible and full of glory" (1 Peter 1:8).

REACHING THE PEAK

Autumn represents the peak of our powers and success in each stage of life.

For instance, in elementary school a boy might be entering his final year with numerous friends, chosen as the assistant captain of the Little League baseball team, and succeeding in the advanced math program.

A teenager may be the star player on the basketball team, taking college level courses, and enjoying popularity among her peers.

Parents come to the point of seeing their children leave home and get married. Grandchildren may even be on the way.

A man may have been promoted to vice president of marketing at the company where he began as a local sales rep. Or a woman may now be running her own successful business.

A retired person might serve on numerous committees at church and also enjoy a fulfilling social life while traveling regularly—with ample time to invest in others' lives.

As we've seen, each time we enter a new stage of life, we pass through the spring entry season as we discover fresh possibilities, meet new friends and colleagues, and undertake diverse endeavors. Then during summer we develop our skills and hone our craft through hard work. But after extensive effort and much learning (sometimes through the school of hard knocks), we eventually master our present role. It's time to reap a harvest. In summer we worked hard; in autumn we should work smart.

Let's revisit four major life areas—identity, relationships, role, and faith—in terms of this magnificent autumn season.

REFLECT AND RESPOND

1. What would you like to see engraved on your tombstone as a summation of what your life on earth accomplished?

2. What do you enjoy most about nature's season of autumn? What do you like least about it?

3. What have been some memorable rewards and accomplishments in your previous autumns (as a season in your stages of life)? How would you describe the inner fulfillment you experienced at those times?

4. What have been your greatest regrets and disappointments as you reached the autumns of your life?

5. How have your summers affected your autumns? What might you do to ensure a greater harvest during the next autumn season of your life?

17

Autumn and Our Identity

Autumn can be deeply rewarding...or painfully disappointing.

Spring, as we've seen, is generally filled with hope and potential. Will I do well in high school and earn a college scholarship? Can I succeed as a salesperson and rise to a management position? Will my kids grow up to become outstanding adults? Not everyone has the same number or quality of opportunities in spring, but we all have the chance to enthusiastically grasp whatever possibilities lie before us.

Summer, as we've seen, is the time to make the most of what we've been given. Did he work hard and become the head of his lawn mowing crew? Did she practice extra hard and become the star of her swim team? Did he read helpful books, attend seminars, ask for advice, and invest himself thoroughly until he became an outstanding father to his two kids?

Fall is when we reap what we've sown. For some, these years are a bountiful harvest, a time to celebrate the success that comes from having done their best. For others, fall is a period of disappointment as they realize they never reached their potential.

Still Growing

Life is about maturing, and our personal growth reaches its peak in autumn. We weren't designed to remain static.

Some people, however, get stuck in a stagnant identity.

My son Mike spent two summers working for the city's grounds-keeping crew. It was a great job for earning college tuition money. Many of the employees were students like Mike. But there were also some "lifers." These were the middle-aged folks who began working for the town right out of high school; sadly, they never moved on.

Now don't get me wrong. There's nothing wrong with doing manual labor or, for that matter, remaining at the same company or the same job for a long period. The problem is that these people had apparently stopped growing. They routinely bragged every Monday morning at coffee break about how wasted they'd been on the weekend. The only change in their stories from week to week was the slang they used to describe the level of intoxication they'd reached. They complained bitterly about management's mundane decisions while seemingly having no greater aspirations in life than holding on until the next weekend's party.

It was as if these individuals had stepped out of high school into a time warp that hurtled them into the future and dumped them out as middle-aged men and women, totally unprepared for their roles as adults.

"When I was a child," the apostle Paul observed, "I spoke as a child, I understood as a child, I thought as a child; but when I became a man, I put away childish things" (1 Corinthians 13:11). We ought to leave a stage of life with more maturity than when we entered!

OUR MOMENT ON THE STAGE

I've already recounted to you my son Daniel's tentative forays into first grade and his morbid fear of show and tell. Fast-forward four years to his fourth grade "graduation." There was a schoolwide program on the final day of school. The fourth graders, standing at the precipice of middle school, were given awards and recognitions as well as a moving speech by the kindhearted principal. Then the stage curtains parted, and there was Daniel with two of his friends dressed like the legendary rocker Alice

Cooper. As Cooper's classic anthem "School's Out" boomed through the loudspeakers, Daniel—impersonating Cooper—began lip-syncing while feverishly playing his cardboard electric guitar.

Daniel? The kid who was prepared to flunk first grade rather than participate in show and tell? Rocking out before the principal, hundreds of parents, and the entire student body? What had happened? Daniel had grown up (if becoming a rock star can be classified as growing up). At center stage on the last day of elementary school, Daniel had peaked (although it had taken awhile).

Each of us should have our moment on the stage when our summer labor reaches its culmination. Autumn is our final "rock concert" before we move on to the next stage of life.

When Preparation Is Proven

Some fall seasons in our lives are more significant than others. Becoming the leading hitter on the Little League baseball team is certainly momentous. But achieving the presidency of the company or walking a daughter down the aisle to marry a godly young man will likely have far greater ramifications in the long run.

Winston Churchill experienced numerous stages throughout his illustrious life. But it was when he reached the peak of his political powers as Britain's prime minister during World War II that he made his greatest and most memorable contribution. Churchill later noted that it was as if his entire life had merely been preparatory for his crowning moment on the world stage.

Other world leaders have suffered character flaws that restricted them from achieving their full potential in autumn. It was said of Richard Nixon that in his rise to the presidency, he mastered everything but himself. Unable to control his feelings of insecurity and innate distrust of others, his paranoia led to the unraveling of his life's greatest achievement.

Whether we're in the stage of high school, marriage, or retirement, our success will inevitably hinge on how prepared we were to grow.

A TIME OF ACCOUNTING

Autumn is many people's favorite season because it allows them to enjoy the fruits of their labors and to experience their just rewards. For others autumn is a time of accounting when they are disappointed by failing to achieve their dreams of spring.

Arthur Miller tells a disturbing story in his classic 1949 play *Death of a Salesman*. The protagonist, a traveling salesman named Willy Loman, dreams of making it big one day. His problem is that he's not very good at sales. Working on commission, he barely ekes out a living. Week after week he hits the road, hoping to drum up more business, then wearily returns to his family on weekends. Frustrated and unhappy, Willy copes with his miserable life by fantasizing that one day everything will be different.

Meanwhile he fabricates wild tales of his success and fame that he tells his son, Biff, who believes him. Willy dreams that Biff will eventually succeed and achieve what he himself failed to accomplish.

At first, Biff is too young and naive to recognize the discrepancy between his father's exotic stories and their impoverished lifestyle. But in time Biff realizes his father is a fraud and leaves home in disgust. His departure compels Willy to perform one last desperate act to help his son achieve the success that eluded him.

Willy's story is of a man reaching autumn and facing the devastating truth that his dreams never became reality.

For decades audiences have been deeply moved by this play. Miller's work presents the haunting specter that we too might fall short of our dreams.

Autumn reveals what we've ultimately become.

REFLECT AND RESPOND

1. How has your sense of identity changed in the previous autumns that you've experienced in earlier stages of your life?

2. What experiences have you had, if any, of being disappointed during an autumn season in your life? What caused this disappointment?

3. What experiences in your life have served most to convince you that we reap what we sow?

4. What is your reaction to the play *Death of a Salesman*? Are there any adjustments you need to make so you don't end your current stage of life in disappointment?

5. Regardless of what season you're in, what is one particular assumption about yourself that you would be wise to examine and reconsider at this time in your life?

18

Our Relationships in Autumn

Our relationships can reach their greatest potential for fulfillment in the days of our autumns, when the seeds sown and the hard work done in our relationships pay their greatest dividends.

Marriage

Autumnal relationships are largely reflections of the work we invested during summer—and marriage is no exception.

A colleague of mine has been married almost thirty years. Ken and Pat have eight children (no twins, no adoptions, and it's not a blended family; they were just prolific). They've come a long way from the starry-eyed college students who got married. Although they've been through some hard times, they're still going strong.

I asked Ken for the secret to their success. In reply he mentioned some great pointers, but it all came down to their attitudes. As Ken expressed it, "I've always told Pat that if she ever leaves me, I'm going with her!"

When Lisa and I were dating, we knew another couple who were constantly talking through their relationship. One of them would raise a concern, big or small, and they would begin discussing it—*vigorously*. A few of their "discussions" registered on the Richter scale.

Being unmarried at the time, Lisa and I weren't always sure what to make of these animated conversations. At times we'd come up with polite excuses to evacuate the premises and leave them to themselves. We earnestly prayed God would at least preserve their volatile marriage until Christmas so their children could have their family intact for the holidays.

Thirty years later their marriage is going stronger than ever. They have a great life together and are thoroughly enjoying their grandkids. And I don't think the credit goes to Lisa's and my intercessory prayers on their behalf. What we realize now, after a few decades of marriage ourselves, is that this couple was constantly working on their relationship. They *communicated*. They brought up problems. They were honest. They worked things out. They forgave and made up. And as each new period of life arrived, they got to work once again and made the most of that stage too.

As unromantic and un-Hollywood as it sounds, the marriage you harvest in autumn always reveals the work you and your spouse invested in summer.

CHILDREN

As I shared earlier, every new stage in your child's life requires a change in your relationship with that child. Succeeding relationally with your preschool daughter sets a great foundation for when she's a teen. But if you don't make adjustments as she enters her next stage of life, you're courting disaster.

The best parents, in my observation, have been those who grew *with* their children. That's why it's harder for absentee parents to stay connected with their families.

I have a job that requires constant travel. Thank heavens for texting, e-mails, and social media. My daughter has a worn-out little bed cushion that I gave her years ago with these words on it: "A daughter is just a little girl who grows up to become a friend."

One caution on that point, however. Parents shouldn't get ahead of themselves either. Some parents treat their preschooler as if he's entitled to the prerogatives of an adult. Or they act as though their child is their best friend. That doesn't generally work. Kids *need* parents. They can always find other friends. They'll generally have only one mom or dad, so parents must fill that crucial role. Once children grow up and become adults, the relationship can transform into a friendship. Nevertheless, you should never completely surrender your role as a parent. Even sixty-year-olds appreciate having a mom or dad to call upon!

My wife has always been an extremely involved, nurturing parent. Because she derived so much joy from caring for our three children, she predictably struggled when Mike, our oldest, began to exercise his independence in his late teens. Mike, like most young adult men, didn't appreciate having his mother remind him to wear his jacket when it got cold so he wouldn't catch pneumonia or to be sure to drink lots of water so he wouldn't get dehydrated. At first Lisa thought he was rejecting her expressions of love when he dismissed her words of maternal concern. But then both Lisa and I came to realize that as our children entered adulthood, we needed to retrofit our relationship from *caregivers* to *consultants*.

This phenomenon manifests itself in many ways, but let me share one example. Growing up, Mike always loved lemon pie. Lisa used to bake him one whenever she sensed he needed a special treat. Mike was nobody's fool. He unashamedly played on his mom's compassionate side more than once to bring on an "oh you poor dear" pie.

Now twenty-seven and living in another state, Mike makes his own desserts. The other day Lisa was delighted when he called to ask her how to make a lemon pie. Their conversation went something like this:

Lisa: Well, first things first. Let's talk about the pastry.

Mike: I've already got that part covered. I bought a ready-made, prebaked crust.

Lisa: Okay, good. Now for the filling you'll need—

Mike: Oh, I bought a mix for the filling. On the box it says you just add milk and stir with a whisk. Except I don't own a whisk. Oh, and I'm out of milk.

Lisa: I gave you two whisks for Christmas. Borrow the milk from your neighbor, who also happens to be your aunt. Now the meringue can be tricky—

Mike: Well, actually, I've never cared for meringue. I'm skipping that part.

Brief pause.

Lisa: Well, Son, it looks like, between the two of us, we've worked out how to make your pie.

Mike: Thanks, Mom! You're the best! I'll let you know how it turns out.

It's *great* being the parent of twenty-somethings. It's just not the same as when you were rearing preschoolers!

Wise parents know to change with the seasons, and along the way they enjoy tender autumn moments with their family.

PARENTS

By the time we become adults, we can assume that whatever relationship we've developed with our parents over the years is now cast in stone. Unfortunately, for some, that relationship continues to bring heartache. The good news is that every time we enter a new stage of our lives, we have the opportunity to restructure all our relationships, including the one with our parents. This is where a seasonal approach to life is especially powerful.

Some people assume that "what will be, will be" and resign themselves to a status quo relationship with their parents or stepparents. After all, how do you change your parents? So a teenager who constantly fought with his father eagerly goes off to college in a distant state and never calls. A woman who was deeply hurt by her mother's criticism moves with her husband hundreds of miles away and rarely returns to visit. A young boy carries deep emotional pain into adulthood because he believes his father was always disappointed in him. Some people feel so grieved over their childhood relationships with their parents that they want nothing more to do with them.

It's appalling what people do to one another and especially how some parents callously treat their children. Yet the writer of Proverbs sagely exhorts, "Let your father and your mother be glad, and let her who bore you rejoice" (23:25). Scripture also says, " 'Honor your father and mother,' which is the first commandment with promise: 'that it may be well with you and you may live long on the earth' " (Ephesians 6:2–3). Tragically this command seems impossible to many disillusioned people.

The later seasons of life can offer hope to people who've been dissatisfied with their family relationships. Some parents were too busy during their working years to actively engage in their children's lives; as a result, their neglected offspring were deeply wounded. Now, in retirement, a parent may finally come to grips with what really matters in life. It would be easy (and seemingly justifiable) for wounded children to grimly turn the table and show Dad or Mom how neglect feels. Or they could seize this fresh stage in life to build a meaningful relationship they never had before.

Some fathers are clueless about how to relate to children, even their own. However, when his son or daughter eventually grows up and enters the work force, the dad might finally feel at ease to relate to them as adults.

My father was away from home a lot speaking at conferences when I was a teenager. When I became an adult, I began speaking with him at some of those events. Those meetings caused extended time away from my dad when I was a child; as adults, however, we had hotel rooms next to each other, ate together in restaurants, and shared the stimulating experience of speaking to large audiences and witnessing people's life-changing encounters with God.

Having entered the career stage of my adult life, I suddenly had the opportunity to know my father in ways that were largely inaccessible to me as a child. As new stages of my career dawned, so did fresh opportunities to relate to my father. It wasn't that my dad loved me any less before I grew up and joined him in ministry. But now we share a bond that has deepened our respect for one another. I'm so grateful for the memories we've been making in this stage of our lives.

Many people find that the arrival of grandchildren opens doors with their parents that were previously closed. Some children work hard during their later summer seasons to build relationships with their parents that they missed during their youth. As a result they experience the intimacy with them as adults that seemed impossible for them as children. Others either don't want to put in the effort or have no hope of change and enter the later stages of their lives without the powerful influence and support from those who gave them life.

As parents enter new stages of life, their children will inevitably have to adjust the way they relate to them. A father may have been a strong, Type A personality who was a superhero to his children. But he's much older now. He doesn't have the strength or energy he once had. Now instead of the father solving his children's problems, he needs his offspring to care for him. A mother may have been a powerful, matriarchal figure who efficiently ran her large home for years. She could pull together enormous family gatherings in her sleep. She made the highly praised Proverbs 31 woman look like a self-centered slouch! But that was years ago. Now she lives in a nursing home, and the scope of her decision making has been drastically reduced.

In both cases these people's children must choose how to refashion their relationships with their aging parents. Do they overlook the inevitably annoying habits that plague the elderly? Do they dismiss their parents as no longer able to make major contributions? Do they lose patience when their parents' memories grow fuzzy and they get their facts wrong or when they get taken in by a telemarketer and buy a time-share in South Dakota?

I love to observe adults patiently including their elderly parents in the life of their family. Women consult with their aged mothers about homemade bread recipes. Sons move their parents into suites attached to their house so they can continue to live semi-independently. Unless we lose our parents to death prematurely, most of us will walk through the bittersweet days of our parents' aging.

I'm currently the president of an organization that my father founded (Blackaby Ministries International—www.blackaby.org), and he's the president emeritus. When people ask me what the president of BMI does, I answer, "Whatever the president emeritus tells him to do!"

My father is the greatest man of God I've ever known (and I've known many). In his day he was a machine. I've never seen anyone work as hard and long as he did. He touched the lives of millions of people. Even as he traveled around the world fulfilling countless speaking engagements, he always had time to stop and listen to people's stories.

But he's presently seventy-seven. He has lost some of his hearing. His arthritic hips are uncomfortable as he walks or gets in and out of vehicles. (I like to tease him that watching him awkwardly getting in or out of a car is "poetry in motion.") Today one of the most agonizing experiences for me—as a driven, Type A personality—is traversing an airport with my father. He makes molasses look like an Olympic track-and-field competitor! And why does he insist on telling the security official checking IDs that I'm his oldest child and that he has four other children and fourteen grandchildren? "Dad! Put your pictures away! Just empty your pockets, and let's get through the x-ray machine!"

Nevertheless, I must constantly remind myself that my father is still a great man of God who's loved by many, including me. So I continue to redesign my relationship with my parents. As a result they continue to bless my life richly.

FRIENDS

To the self-centered, friends are people who show kindness to you, such as helping you move into a new apartment, giving you a lift home when your car's in the shop, or inviting you to their parties. But really, friends are primarily the people in whom *you* have invested. Each stage of life offers a plethora of opportunities for meeting people and helping to improve their lives in some way. The new relationship may be a sixth-grade classmate, a professional colleague, a young mother at your church, or a fellow golfer in your retirement community.

One of the greatest privileges people have during their brief sojourn through life is the chance to exert a positive impact on the lives of a few others along the way. Whether you live selfishly or selflessly, autumn reveals the fruitfulness or barrenness of your relationships. I once read of someone who claimed his goal in life was to have at least one person sit through his funeral without looking at his watch!

Recently I was speaking at a conference in North Carolina. As the sound technician hooked up my microphone, he told me he had a message for me. Apparently his father had heard that I was coming to his son's church and told him a story. Fifty years earlier the man was starting out as a pastor in Los Angeles and feeling overwhelmed by his task. He needed someone to help him learn how to minister in that challenging urban setting. He recalled that my father (who was a young pastor himself at the time) consistently encouraged him and made a special effort to help him. Later, when the young clergyman was admitted into the intensive care unit at the local hospital, my father was the only person outside his family who visited him. Now, half a century later, this man wanted his son to tell me how much he appreciated the investment my father had made at a critical juncture in his life.

That same weekend one of the staff members at the church where I was speaking told me about a tragic auto accident involving her family. Her brother-in-law and his young son had been killed, while another son, an infant, was critically injured and airlifted to a hospital in Dallas. The family frantically gathered at the hospital to wait and pray. Someone who knew the family had heard my dad was in Dallas leading a conference that week, so she sent word to him about the accident.

During a break in the conference, my dad excused himself from his hosts and went to the hospital to comfort these people, whom he'd never met. The grieving family was in shock but deeply touched when my father arrived unexpectedly and helped them experience the peace of God in the midst of their pain.

Since my father's name is well known in many Christian denominations, I hear numerous accounts like these. In a Christian bookstore recently, the clerk noticed my last name on my credit card. "Any relation to Henry?" she asked, and I knew a story was coming. A dozen years earlier she was part of a group studying *Experiencing God.* During that time one of the members was devastated after suffering a miscarriage. The bereft young woman couldn't fathom how a loving God would allow such a tragedy. The store clerk told me she'd written a letter to my father and addressed it to the large ministry office in Atlanta where he worked. She wanted him to pray for this grieving mother, though neither woman knew him personally. My father's office staff tracked down the bereaved young woman's phone number (at a time before Google), and my dad called her. Over the phone he led her in a calming, encouraging time of prayer.

Once again I was asked to tell my dad that his words had brought peace and comfort to an aching heart. The woman's faith was renewed, and she subsequently gave birth to several beautiful children.

My father is known for writing books and speaking to large audiences. But lately I've realized that he has primarily impacted others by simply doing what we all should do—take time to care about people.

When you choose to invest in people's lives throughout summer, you'll leave an autumn legacy of encouragement. Whether you ever hear about it or not, people will be profoundly grateful that your path crossed with theirs.

REFLECT AND RESPOND

1. How easily and readily can you celebrate when others are experiencing autumn harvests in their lives?

2. How can you encourage people who are facing an autumn that will produce a small or nonexistent harvest due to their own choices?

3. What are some of the greatest benefits you've experienced from an extended, maturing relationship?

4. Think about your relationships with your spouse, children, friends, and colleagues. What's something you might do to encourage and bless each one? If your parents are still living, what is your relationship like with them? Is there anything you could do to improve it?

5. Do you know of someone close to you who is currently in an autumn season? How can you encourage this person with something you've learned so far from this book?

19

Our Roles in Autumn

If spring is when we take on new roles and summer is when we work hard and advance in those assignments, autumn is when we master our tasks and reach the limits of our skills and influence. We're no longer desperately trying to learn our jobs; they are now old hat. Whether we're navigating our way through high school, parenting our children, or trying to succeed at business, teaching, or practicing medicine, we know what we're doing. (At least we think we do!)

Often this is the time when we achieve levels of greater responsibility—say, as captain of the soccer team or as a charge nurse or as partner in a law firm or as a regional manager at the company. This is potentially when our lives have their greatest impact on others.

Seth Godin describes people who are performing their jobs at the optimum level as linchpins, because they're the last people a company wants to see go.[21] Whether it's the person everyone depends on at the company, the mother who keeps the family going, or the church member who seems to be needed on every committee, people find their purpose for that autumn stage of their lives, and they make the most of it.

Autumn Moments in History

I love history. For some, history is nothing more than dry, dusty facts about people who died a long time ago or about events that hardly matter anymore. But history describes people who made a difference in their world, and autumn is the season when they typically impacted history the most.

Politicians such as Abraham Lincoln and Winston Churchill achieved their highest office during the autumn of their lives.[22] Because of the wisdom they gained through their failures and setbacks of summer, these men rose above their peers during national crises.

I also think of women like Susannah Wesley. The last of twenty-five children herself, she gave birth to nineteen of her own, eleven of whom did not survive her. Enduring numerous hardships, including two house fires, poverty, and more than a yearlong absence of her husband, Susannah diligently taught all her children and brought them up in the fear of the Lord. Deeply impacted by their mother's teachings and writings, her two sons John and Charles eventually founded the Methodist Church and were used by God as pioneers in a movement of spiritual revival that swept England in the late 1700s.

Then there was Queen Elizabeth I, who donned armor and rode to encourage her troops as the invincible Spanish Armada approached, a critical turning point in history that would propel England into centuries of greatness as a world power.[23] This moment of glory and fulfillment came some thirty years into her reign; thirty years of summer labor had been spent in wise governance based on good counsel and careful moderation amid troubling circumstances. The harvest for her labor was a newly invigorated nation, ready to assume inspired leadership on the world stage.

Or consider inventor and businessman Thomas Edison. Edison exemplified hard summer work in applying his gifted mind to a wide variety of practical needs and problems in the world around him, always with the intent of finding something new he could manufacture. As a result, he eventually held nearly eleven hundred patents in the United States (and others in Europe). The majority of these were for inventions or much-needed improvements related to electric light and power (including his most famous contribution: a practical, long-lasting light bulb), the phonograph, the telegraph, alkaline storage batteries, and the telephone. In addition, because of his camera inventions and improvements, Edison is considered the founder of the motion-picture industry. All told, his work made him the most important figure in laying the foundation for the modern electric-powered world.

Edison had a knack and a driving ambition for mass-producing workable versions of his inventions that could easily be put into the service of mankind. Along with his entrepreneurial accomplishments (he was the founder of General Electric and a dozen other companies), his tireless pursuit of life-enhancing inventions led to a transformation of daily life for the average citizen. That was the major harvest of his autumn, the fruit of his endless hours of summer labor.

Edison was famous for his tireless persistence and positive attitude, as shown in his countless failed attempts before he finally crafted a more practical light bulb. Rather than being discouraged by such failures, he knew that "every wrong attempt discarded is another step forward."[24]

It's not that such hard work came easily to him. Over his desk he displayed this quotation from Joshua Reynolds: "There is no expedient to which a man will not resort to avoid the real labor of thinking."[25] Edison committed himself to that very "real labor of thinking," and within his lifetime won legendary status and a lasting place in history for his practical service to humanity.

In every field surveyed by history—from politics to the military, from the arts to science and commerce—people have reached the peak of their influence and achieved their greatest performances in autumn. As a result the world has changed.

February 23, 1807, was one of those watershed moments in history. William Wilberforce had been fighting for the abolition of the slave trade in England for two decades. He'd been continually ostracized and mocked by his colleagues for his seemingly prudish approach to business and his unwillingness to leave well enough alone (the slave trade, after all, was profitable for a great many people in Britain). But when the abolition bill passed into law, Wilberforce sat weeping as the crowning achievement of his life occurred before his very eyes. Spontaneously members of the House of Commons rose to their feet and cheered for the diminutive politician who had shunned the opportunity for the highest office in order to invest his life in a higher good.[26]

AUTUMN INVESTMENTS

During spring and summer we may get advice from others that can help us in our role. But in autumn it's our turn to invest in others. This is the time to motivate the rookies on our high school football team, or to encourage young parents or newlyweds, or to mentor junior colleagues at work, or to disciple new believers at our church. People around us recognize that we've achieved success in our fields and now have wisdom that could enable others to succeed as well.

Of course, this scenario doesn't describe everyone in autumn. Some people didn't put in adequate effort during summer, or they made foolish choices, and now in autumn their harvest is barren.

It's sad when people desperately want to be promoted into a management position or to be sought out for advice or enlisted to write a book but those who observe their lives find nothing attractive. They're like the woman who felt well qualified to offer marital advice to others since she herself had been divorced five times. Or they're like the minister who sought to counsel others on pastoral leadership based on his being fired from his last four ecclesiastical positions.

Almost nothing gives people more influence in autumn than a successful track record in summer.

AUTUMNAL SUCCESS

As I've mentioned, my work includes the privilege of ministry partnership with a unique group of Christian executives. These men and women live in cities all over America, and their personalities are as diverse as the corporations they lead. The common denominator is their desire to honor God by making a positive difference in their respective worlds.

One of these people is Dick Schultz. This successful man was born in 1929 in Kellogg, Iowa. In college he excelled in three sports and signed a contract to play professional baseball. However, his real passion was for teaching and coaching, so he opted to become a high school biology teacher and coach instead.

Recognized for his accomplishments at the high school level, Dick was later invited to coach baseball and later basketball at the University of Iowa. After a successful coaching career, he was hired as the athletic director for Cornell University and later for the University of Virginia. As a highly regarded coach in collegiate sports, he was hired by the NCAA in 1987 to be its second executive director. He purchased a Learjet (which he flew himself) and spent two hundred days a year traveling to colleges and universities nationwide.

In 1995, at age sixty-six, Dick Schultz stepped down from leading the NCAA. Rather than retire, however, he moved on to become the executive director of the US Olympic Committee and was involved in planning Olympic Games. In 2000, at seventy-one, he retired from this position. Still not one to slow down, he then began an international marketing company.

Today at age eighty-three, Dick draws on his vast experience to mentor CEOs of major companies. In addition, he has established similar support networks of Christian CEOs in Asia.

I regularly work alongside Dick, providing training sessions for Christian CEOs. Two years ago he invited me to speak at a conference he'd organized in Hong Kong. One afternoon he took me on a walking tour of the city's downtown. He's more than thirty years my senior, and I could barely keep up with him!

What motivates busy CEOs around the world to make time to meet with Dick? They respect him as a professional, and they know they can learn from his wide-ranging experience. Dick is a refined and unpretentious man. He jokes that he's so old he's stopped buying green bananas! Yet he has enjoyed success in every stage of his life. He has navigated a variety of spring seasons in his life…and has also enjoyed numerous bumper crops in autumn.

Because the stages of life tend to build one upon another, those who develop successful track records enjoy a widening influence throughout their lives.

REFLECT AND RESPOND

1. Of all the most important roles in your life, in which ones, if any, are you now experiencing an autumn season, a time of reaping the results of past labor?

2. Looking back on your past, in what ways have your roles developed in the autumn seasons you've known, the harvest times of your previous labor?

3. In what roles do you sense that you've achieved mastery or the peak of your abilities? Where do you have the strongest track records?

4. What are some accomplishments you had hoped for in your life that you haven't yet experienced? Do you need to relinquish any of those dreams? Or are there adjustments and efforts you could make that might help you ultimately achieve them?

5. If you're presently in an autumn season of life, how are you encouraging and blessing others through your experience, wisdom, and success?

20

Autumn and Our Faith

When people are born again, they begin their Christian lives as spiritual infants. However, God gives us numerous opportunities to grow and mature in our faith. This spiritual development comes through reading, believing, and obeying the Bible. It also results from prayer, being actively involved in a local church, and participating in Bible studies, worship, and mission endeavors.

Of course, spiritual strength and maturity stem from choices we make. There are no divine steroids. After neglecting your spiritual food and exercise, you can't then rush the growth process by attending a weekend-long Christian conference. Spiritual development occurs like physical growth—by regularly practicing good habits.

I had the privilege of updating and revising my father's classic book *Experiencing God.*[27] Over the years I've been amazed to hear people testify how the biblical truths found in that book have helped their faith expand beyond anything they could have imagined. After reading the material, one woman was motivated to open an orphanage in Africa. Numerous people sensed God leading them to plant new churches. One man started a business that became a platform for spreading the gospel. Another reader began a soup kitchen for the homeless. Several entered politics. Many have written books.

These people realized God was initiating a brand-new spring season

in their lives. They accepted God's invitation (though they were sometimes scared to death) and began to obey—one step at a time—what
God told them to do in summer. By the time these people reached
autumn, they were brimming with stories about their amazing journeys.

What a pleasure to hear how God used ordinary people to accomplish the extraordinary!

TRUSTING GOD FOR MIGHTY MEN

While visiting Africa in May 2010, I met Angus Buchan, a man with
quite a story. Of Scottish descent, Angus was a farmer in Zambia. But
due to political unrest there, in 1978 he migrated hundreds of miles south
to Greytown, South Africa. The move brought a new spring season into
Buchan's life—an opportunity to start over in more ways than one.

He was working hard, trying to eke out a modest living for himself
and his family in the face of numerous challenges that always seemed
on the verge of ruining him. Amid these difficulties Angus and his wife,
Jill, turned their lives over to Christ in 1979. The next year they sensed
that God was giving them a threefold vision for their lives: first, the Great
Commission to share the gospel (Mark 16:15); second, caring for
orphans and widows (James 1:27); and third, equipping other believers
for the work of ministry (Ephesians 4:12).

In 1989 Angus rented a town hall and inauspiciously launched his
preaching ministry. In 1995 the Buchans began a home for orphans on
their property called Beth-Haitlaim (a Hebrew term meaning "house
of lambs"). Throughout the summer season of their new ministry, the
Buchans preached and served wherever they had the opportunity.

In 2004, Angus launched a new ministry on his property called the
Mighty Men Conference. Angus sensed that the white men of South
Africa were disillusioned and searching for answers. He issued a call for
them to return to God in revival and to rise up as mighty men for God's
purposes. In 2004, at the first of a series of annual conferences at his little

farm in rural northeastern South Africa, two hundred men showed up. By 2007, there were seventy-four hundred. In 2008, sixty thousand men arrived. Then in April 2009, South Africa gasped as over two hundred thousand men came to hear Angus preach four times over the weekend. Men traveled as far as five hundred miles to attend. People brought their own bedding, food, and even chairs to sit on. During the meetings there was a huge groundswell of commitment by those in attendance to take their faith in God to a higher level.

Angus decided to have one final Mighty Men Conference in April 2010. But on the morning people were scheduled to arrive, he began having second thoughts. He worried that perhaps he'd finally overreached himself.

He climbed a hillside on his property and began to pray and ask God to give him a sign if indeed he was supposed to hold this Mighty Men Conference. He suddenly heard a humming sound. At first, he thought it was a swarm of insects. But as he looked to the east, he noticed a long line of vehicles stretching into the horizon as far as he could see. They were making their way to his farm. Angus glanced to the west and noticed another distant line of vehicles approaching his property. When the meeting began, more than three hundred thousand men had gathered to hear what the farmer with a modest education had to say.

As Buchan told me this story, he was overcome with emotion. He knew he'd experienced firsthand what almighty God can do with an ordinary life that's wholly surrendered to Him. He was a transplanted farmer with a meager education and no formal ministerial training, yet the Lord used him to challenge hundreds of thousands of men from across his country.

For years Angus had faithfully served God in summer, speaking in town halls and to small gatherings. But the Mighty Men Conferences represented his autumn, the harvest of all his labors. People recognized that this farmer had a word from God, and they were prepared to travel great distances to hear what he had to say.

BITTERSWEET AUTUMNS

Autumn can be bittersweet. For even as we reach the height of our powers, a decline may already be setting in. As we lead our high school basketball team in scoring, we realize that we'll soon be going to college, where we're uncertain if we can even make the team. In professional hockey, winning Coach of the Year is almost synonymous with being fired the following season. Even the most prolific hitters in baseball eventually see their batting averages slip. Undefeated boxers inevitably meet their match. Nothing lasts forever.

For Samuel L. Clemens—the author famously known as Mark Twain—the year 1885 raised him to spectacular heights in American culture. His masterpiece, *The Adventures of Huckleberry Finn,* was published that year. Meanwhile he embarked on a Twins of Genius tour with his friend and fellow author George Washington Cable, in which the two literary celebrities spoke to more than a hundred appreciative audiences across North America.

He was at the peak of his fame, he had the love of his wife and three daughters, and he anticipated achieving financial security. He was investing heavily in a new typesetting machine that promised to earn him an immense fortune. Twain seemed at this time, as his biographer states, to be "indomitable, a god of his century." But he had reached an apex, and this fruitful autumn would be brief, followed soon by severe disappointments. This famous man "had no way of knowing that his greatest work was now behind him, and that the fortune churning his way would be ground to dust.... In his final quarter century, life would never again be quite as sweet for Samuel Langhorne Clemens as it was at this moment."[28]

Twain's publishing company would eventually go bankrupt, the typesetting business he invested in would prove to be a bust, and he would be forced to live in exile in Europe for a decade to restore his finances. He would also lose his beloved wife Livy and two of his three daughters to illness. Twain would eventually experience a new spring season but only after an unusually long and harsh winter.

WHAT NEXT?

The uncertainty of what will come next adds drama to autumn. Even as we win awards and enjoy promotions and recognition, there's an eerie awareness that, having reached the pinnacle of that stage of life, there's only one direction for us to go next. And that direction is downward.

Some fortunate people manage to remain at the top for unusually long periods of time, but eventually, like conquerors of Mount Everest, we take a deep breath, celebrate our feat, take a few moments to enjoy the spectacular view, and then commence our inevitable decline.

The key to autumn is not living gloomily, desperately clutching whatever trophies or positions we managed to collect along the way. For even though we cannot live in perpetual harvest, we can rest assured that a new spring will eventually come.

But before our next spring dawns, we must undergo the most universally feared season of all: *winter*. Let's step forward bravely and explore what this final season is all about.

REFLECT AND RESPOND

1. Even skilled and seasoned farmers sometimes experience crop failure due to circumstances outside their control. Have there been similar results in an autumn season in your life, despite your efforts and experience?

2. What habits in your spiritual life do you see as most important for the long haul—for bringing the most spiritual benefit in the coming decades of your life?

3. Looking back on your life and on what you've accomplished, what are you most grateful to God for? How does this kind of gratitude strengthen your faith?

4. What is something God has done in your life that has caught you by surprise or amazed you? (If you're unable to think of anything, what might that suggest to you?)

21

WINTER: THE TIME OF ENDINGS

My two sons shared many of the same dreams. Both envisioned becoming Ninja Turtles; both thought they were second cousins, twice removed, to Luke Skywalker (on his father's side); and both imagined themselves becoming hockey legends (or at least as good as their dad). But undoubtedly the shared dream that trumped all others—and came closest to becoming reality—was that of being rock stars.

ONE BAND'S FLING

Their fantasy began innocuously. Mike, at age fifteen, quietly laid aside his clarinet (few sounds rival the melodic delight of a freshmen band concert boasting a sizable clarinet section!), and picked up a pair of drumsticks. Daniel abandoned his band instrument (I'm not sure what it was called, but it resembled a sawed-off tuba) and embraced the electric guitar. A legend was born.

Their musical talents remained largely unrecognized until they entered a talent competition at a local high school. The boys recruited additional band members for the contest and launched the high-energy, head-banging rock band known as Fading Rebel.

They were among a number of interesting acts entered in the Battle of the Bands that evening, but the only serious competition was a cover band for the Rolling Stones. When the Mick Jagger look-alike began prancing across the stage, throwing his shirt into the crowd, and singing, "I can't get no satisfaction," my boys thought they might have met their match. But when the dust settled and the ballots were counted, Fading Rebel had won its first music competition.

Buoyed by their astounding success, the band entered a talent contest sponsored by the Calgary Stampede (one of the largest rodeos in North America). Once again, the Rolling Stones were their nemesis. To the delight of their burgeoning fan base (the band members all had supportive families), Fading Rebel sent Mick Jagger and company packing once again and advanced into the second round.

This initial success also earned them the right to perform live on the grounds (at a spot strategically located between the cotton candy booth and an ATM machine). Unfortunately, Fading Rebel was no match for a highland dance troupe and a mother-daughter country singing duo. Its brief but spectacular run in the Stampede talent show came to an abrupt halt.

That minor defeat, however, was far from the end. The band was now on a mission. They began writing their own music. They bought better instruments. They let their hair grow out and even got a few piercings.

It wasn't long before they were invited to play in the Underground, a grungy nightclub for young people, along with various local acts that were better known. After the profanity-laced, head-banging, substance-using opening band had "performed," Fading Rebel appeared onstage for their first paying gig. Fans swarmed the mosh pit shouting enthusiastically (to their siblings in the band), and the concert commenced.

Fading Rebel knew this could be the turning point, the moment that later documentaries and biographers would identify as the pivotal event that catapulted the previously unknown band into the fame and fortune that would eventually be theirs. My boys put on a show for the ages.

Daniel gyrated so energetically he had to ice his neck for days afterward. Mike leaped from the large amplifier. Both boys poured more energy into their songs than Wile E. Coyote uses to chase the Road Runner. Everyone who was asked (and they *were* asked) claimed that the performance was a resounding success.

Other invitations soon followed. The Underground asked them to return (and to bring back their family and friends from church). They were invited to open for an edgy rock band that was touring the area. Fading Rebel hit the road, loading up two vehicles and traveling to various cities to share their musical message. Proceeds from their performances grew, along with their fan base. Unfortunately, corresponding increases in both fuel prices and McDonalds Happy Meals ate away their profits. But their experience was gratifying.

As with many legendary rock bands, tensions developed in Fading Rebel. There were disagreements concerning the direction of their music, how to handle earnings (once they surpassed the cost of fast-food drive-throughs), and differing commitment levels to the band's future. Eventually Fading Rebel faded away, with members pursuing independent musical careers. All that remained were the memories, the privately recorded CDs, and the unsold T-shirts.

Franklin Roosevelt once said that "each age is a dream dying, or one that is coming to birth." At the time of its final concert, Fading Rebel was unaware that this was the end. There were occasional appeals for a reunion tour, but it was clear that winter had descended on the band. Its members moved on.

Today both my sons still use their musical gifts. Mike is the college minister at First Baptist Church in Jonesboro, Georgia, and he's also the lead drummer for the orchestra. He also regularly plays drums or guitar at a young adult coffee shop called Café on Main. Branching out, he's published his first book (the one coauthored with Daniel that I mentioned earlier: *When Worlds Collide*), and he's in a PhD program. And Daniel now plays in a worship band at Epic Church in San Francisco (although he no longer utilizes his head-banging talents). Clearly life moved on.

As their parents, Lisa and I are glad they had their rock star fling. That's what spring is for—developing and pursuing dreams. Sometimes springtime dreams actually work out. The reason many people have midlife crises is due in part because they neglected their dreams and were haunted later in life as they wondered, *What if?* Mike and Daniel won't have to speculate. They had some success (people still view their material at their old website). They enjoyed those times.

We're proud of them for having put in so much effort. (I'm looking forward to hearing what *their* teenage kids think about their parents' antics on stage when they watch the videos.) But we're also proud of them for knowing when to walk away.

No matter how delightful our springs, how industrious our summers, or how profitable our autumns, when winter arrives, it's time to pack up our equipment, put away our warm-weather clothes, and embrace the approaching changes.

Winter is when life says good-bye to what we've known...as it prepares us for the spring that's coming.

The Picture for Us in Nature

Winter is generally the least popular of the four seasons. It has a prevailing sense of barrenness. The leaves have fled the scene. Any fowl holding a valid passport has relocated to warmer locales. The color and perfume of flowers are largely gone, and in their place is a democratizing blanket of snow or listless grass and evergreens.

Few things in nature are as grimly foreboding as winter's severe weather. In some regions it entails months of clouds and rain with scant sunshine. In the north, snowstorms strike with such severity that normal life grinds to a halt, and it seems as if no creature in the wild could possibly survive nature's fury. Temperatures can plummet so low that the air takes your breath away and freezes human flesh on contact. I spent four years living in Winnipeg, Canada (widely known as Winterpeg). One winter, temperatures dipped to minus forty degrees every day for more than a month.

Long gone are summer's tank tops, shorts, and sandals; out come the heavy parkas, scarves, mittens, boots, and of course toques, if you live in Canada (hats or toboggans if you live in the United States).

Winter affects people, and the more winter you experience each year, the greater impact it has. Sociologists have postulated about the differences between people who live in predominantly warm climates and those who inhabit cold regions. Among those who spend a large percentage of the year wearing multiple layers of clothing and covering their heads with hats and scarves, there's often a more reserved approach to interpersonal relationships than there is among people who can wear sandals, T-shirts, and cutoffs year round. In fact, entire books have been written to describe disparities between Americans and Canadians (written by Canadians, who seem more intrigued by the issue). The size of the countries and their respective histories play important roles in creating the differences, but part of the divergence is due to one being a cold country and the other being much warmer.

At the University of Saskatchewan, where Lisa and I attended college, students called February "suicide month" because of its grim death toll. The winter blues are partly the result of a lack of sunlight during those months, which causes many people to experience a form of depression called SAD (Seasonal Affective Disorder). This can be treated by sitting frequently under a sunlamp—and further alleviated by vacationing in Florida or going on Caribbean cruises.

Winter's frigid weather and long, bitterly cold nights drive people inside, where they may feel imprisoned by the cold and isolated from other people. (These feelings may be magnified if one lives in a small home with a large number of rambunctious children.)

Winter is also mysterious, dominated by long shadows and darkness.

The vegetation can be sparse and desolate. Winter's quiet stillness may be hauntingly foreboding. The poet Robert Frost captured something of this specter in his famous poem "Stopping by Woods on a Snowy Evening," with its oft-quoted lines:

> The woods are lovely, dark, and deep,
> But I have promises to keep.

Winter is a paradox. While it may appear as if all life forms have evacuated the premises, close examination reveals abundant activity throughout nature. Animals create minihighways in the snow. There's the cackle of hardy birds defying the elements that try to silence their songs. And though temperatures plummet and the nights are long and dark, the sun can still shine in the daytime and reflect in blinding brilliance off the snow.

People find numerous creative ways to thrive in winter. There are, in fact, many pleasures that are experienced only during this season. Snow sports such as hockey, downhill and cross-country skiing, figure skating, ice fishing, snowmobiling, and curling (a sport many Americans grow fascinated with every Winter Olympics) entertain northerners during winter's gloomy months. School grounds are dotted with sleds and snow forts and "king of the mountain" Armageddons.

Winter can be a time of retrenchment, hibernation, and reflection. Fields that produced enormous harvests during autumn now lie empty as the ground gathers the strength and reserves to return to productivity in spring. Many plants and animals adopt states of dormancy, suspending activity to survive the cold and conserve energy. Animals adapt in a variety of ways, both internally and externally. The bodies of some creatures adjust chemically by producing an "antifreeze" chemical or by slowing down their body functions. Others grow thicker coats. Certain birds will snow roost, taking shelter under a cover of snow that holds warmer air beneath it. Dormant or hibernating mammals store body fat so they don't have to forage in the cold for food. Some rodents and snakes live communally to conserve warmth.

Winter certainly has its unique appeal. Can you imagine anything more innately appealing than being comfortably seated before a warm, crackling fireplace during a cold winter's night? A plush chair, a good book, a steaming cup of hot chocolate, and the flames hypnotically radiating light and warmth—all resonate with our fundamental need for restoration and comfort.

Winter is when we rest and recuperate from demanding summers and autumns in preparation for the coming spring. While there may still be work to do (especially if you raise livestock rather than crops), this is generally a time of withdrawal and reflection. There can be a tinge of sadness to winter as we think back over the periods of growth and harvest that are now past.

THE PICTURE FOR US IN SCRIPTURE

There are numerous examples in the Bible of people who experienced a winter season as they came to the end of a particular stage in their lives. Let's look at two that hold many profound lessons for us.

Perhaps the epitome of a winter season is reflected in the prayerful words of Jesus in John 17. His words to His Father include powerful summary statements of what had happened during the spring, summer, and fall of His public ministry:

> "I have *glorified You* on the earth. I have *finished the work* which
>   You have given Me to do" (verse 4).
> "I have *manifested Your name* to the men whom You have given
>   Me" (verse 6).
> "I have *given to them the words which You have given Me*"
>   (verse 8).

"While I was with them in the world, I *kept them in Your name*"
    (verse 12).

"Those whom You gave Me I have *kept;* and none of them is lost"
    (verse 12).

"I have *given them Your word*" (verse 14).

"As You sent Me into the world, I also have *sent them into the
    world*" (verse 18).

The Savior's earthly ministry to His disciples was drawing to a close,
a ministry fulfilled to perfection—pursued in complete obedience and
accomplished in total dependence on His Father. The fruit of that labor
was represented in the disciples whose lives had been transformed and
who had come to understand the greatest truth of all. Jesus affirmed it in
these ways to His Father:

"They have kept Your word" (verse 6).

"They have known that all things which You have given Me are
    from You" (verse 7).

"They…have known surely that I came forth from You; and they
    have believed that You sent Me" (verse 8).

"I am glorified in them" (verse 10).

"They are not of the world, just as I am not of the world" (verse 16).

You and I can also use our winter seasons to prayerfully reflect on
what has been accomplished in our lives—to see and understand it all
with heightened clarity and appreciation.

The full content of John 17, so rich with the profound prayer requests
of Jesus, shows us that we, too, can use our winter seasons as a special
time of entreaty before God, lifting up our requests especially for the new
stages of life still to come. We can intercede in particular for those we
touched during earlier seasons, just as Jesus prayed not only on behalf of

His disciples, preparing them for their challenging days to come, but also on behalf of *all* believers for all ages—for whom He would die on the cross on the very next day after this prayer was uttered.

Another definitive winter season is reflected in Paul's words in 2 Timothy 4. After so many years of a demanding yet fruitful ministry, the apostle was languishing in a Roman prison, certain that his days on earth were drawing to a close. "The time of my departure is at hand," he told Timothy, and he spoke of "being poured out as a drink offering" (verse 6). These words show us that winter's decline can represent a time of intense devotion and ultimate purpose.

As Paul reflected on the seasons gone by, he was able to reach some comprehensive conclusions: "I have fought the good fight, I have finished the race, I have kept the faith" (verse 7). Nothing brings greater comfort in our winters than to know we lived life well in our earlier seasons, making the most of the opportunities and callings and responsibilities that God brought our way.

Yet Paul was also supremely future focused in this winter hour. "Finally," he said to Timothy, "there is laid up for me the crown of righteousness, which the Lord, the righteous Judge, will give to me on that Day, and not to me only but also to all who have loved His appearing" (verse 8). Our winters' reflections can point us to our future hope, especially to the greatest hope of all.

Underappreciated

Although winter seems for many to be merely a time of isolation, harsh weather, and treacherous travel, the truth is that it serves a crucial role. In fact, winter is probably the most underappreciated season.

God never declares that winter is a vehicle of divine judgment or punishment. Rather, He has designed winter to serve us in valuable ways.

Let's reflect on the four major categories of life and see what winter means for you.

REFLECT AND RESPOND

1. What do you enjoy most about nature's season of winter? What do you like least about it?

2. How well do you handle endings? Are you happy to see them come, or do you dread and resist them?

3. What have you learned so far about successfully bringing stages of your life to a healthy close?

4. What has been the most painful winter in your life so far? Which has been the most rewarding?

22

WINTER AND OUR IDENTITY

We've seen how our identity develops and matures through each period of life. Spring is when we take a fresh look at who we are. During summer, our character grows and is refined. Autumn is when we reach the peak of that stage of life.

Finally, winter draws each stage of life to a close.

I'm a pack rat. I like to get all the mileage I can out of my possessions, and I hate disposing of anything I might need later. Lisa, on the other hand, thinks it's immoral to retain anything you haven't used in the last year when there are so many people who could use it. She keeps a Goodwill box by our back door at all times. She makes scavenging trips through our family's closets looking for items that have dared to collect dust. (She especially delights in pillaging *my* closet when she thinks my business trips have been unnecessarily long.) Lisa argues that before we buy another shirt or pair of pants or DVD, we should make room for the new purchase by giving away something of similar bulk.

This practice also applies to our identity. Something in us may have to die in order to make room for new growth. If it doesn't, our identity becomes congested and cluttered.

The apostle Paul put it this way: "If anyone is in Christ, he is a new creation; *old things have passed away;* behold, all things have become new"

(2 Corinthians 5:17). Problems happen when we keep filling up our lives without first removing debris.

Unwilling to Let Go

This tendency to hold on explains why middle-aged adults sometimes act childishly or why normally generous people become selfish about certain possessions. The unwillingness to let go of the old also explains why highly respected professionals who routinely manage large staffs and close major deals become insanely competitive and rude during games at family gatherings. These people may have taken on adult responsibilities, but they never put to death the fiercely competitive spirit they developed while playing Monopoly with their older siblings as children.

Children are naturally self-centered. As we grow older, we know we need to be more thoughtful of others, so we try to add thoughtfulness to our character repertoire. But most of us still maintain vast reservoirs of egotism that have never died. We live like Dr. Jekyll and Mr. Hyde; people never know which one will show up at any given moment.

Some people decide to start a diet to lose weight. Great! But their fundamental problem is not their weight but the fact that they prize food too highly. Even while on diets, they obsess about food. Perhaps they grew up in homes where food was a reward; whenever they celebrated an accomplishment, they were granted their favorite dessert or a trip to a special restaurant. What they really need to do is put to death the idea that food is a cherished prize. They need to see it for what it is: fuel and potentially a whole lot of calories that will eventually end up on their hips. When they put to death their outdated view of food, dieting won't be as difficult. But as long as they simply *add* a diet to a life that overvalues good-tasting food, dieting will always be a battle (and usually a losing one).

We have a lot of attitudes and viewpoints that may need to die. The list can go on and on.

FREE TO LIVE

I once spoke at a conference about the immeasurable love God has for us. Afterward, during an interactive session, a woman in her fifties stood up and asked to share something with the group. She related that when she was fifteen, her adulterous father abandoned their family. This woman couldn't understand how her father could love her and yet abandon her. She assumed it must be her fault. She viewed herself as so unlovable that even her own father wanted nothing to do with her. Resolving to change the situation, she worked hard to earn straight A's in school. She dressed sharp and excelled in everything she did. She regularly wrote to her father and pleaded for his attention but to no avail.

Eventually she married a fine man and gave birth to two lovely children. But she continued to view herself as unlovely and unlovable. She lived in constant fear that one day her husband would discover how awful she really was and then abandon her, just as her father had done. She feared that her children would do the same thing. So she prepared for the worst. She built a wall between herself and her husband so she would suffer only minimal damage when he eventually abandoned her. She kept her children and friends at a safe distance. She wasn't going to be ambushed the way her mother had been.

During the conference this hurting woman saw for the first time what she'd been doing. Although she had added a husband, children, and friends to her life, she had never allowed outdated and unhealthy views of herself to undergo a much-needed crucifixion. Her husband showered her with affection, her children loved her, her friends had reached out to her, but her false sense of worthlessness had been robbing her of the meaningful life she could have been enjoying.

Before she shared her story with us, this woman had telephoned her husband and tearfully apologized for how she had treated him. She didn't even wait until the end of the conference to return home, so eager was she to rejoin her family and to experience the life she was finally free to enjoy.

In the same way that Lisa unclutters my family's closets and shelves, so we also need to constantly sort through the outdated, immature, or faulty attitudes and character traits that hold us back from thriving in our current stages of life.

So ask yourself: *What opinions, attitudes, characteristics, and behaviors must die in my life so that I'm free to really live?*

REFLECT AND RESPOND

1. Is it easy for you to let go when it's time to move on? Or do you tend to have a hard time doing this?

2. How has your sense of identity changed in the previous winters that you've experienced in earlier stages of your life?

3. How would you answer the concluding question in this chapter: "What opinions, attitudes, characteristics, and behaviors must die in my life so that I'm free to really live?"

4. Do you have any bad habits that have plagued your life for years? Is there any immaturity in your life that should have been dealt with years ago?

5. What is an area of your character that has not matured over the years as it should have? How has this immaturity affected your life?

23

OUR RELATIONSHIPS IN WINTER

Contrary to what some of us have been taught, not all relationships are meant to last forever. Yet if there's anything we feel we *ought* to hold on to, it's our relationships.

PEOPLE CHANGE

Here's a rule of thumb for you: if you haven't changed since you were a teenager, then your best friends from high school probably still have a lot in common with you, assuming they haven't changed either. The truth is, however, people grow, change, and mature.

Now more than ever, our jobs and life changes can transport us thousands of miles away from old friends. Our values and perspectives on life develop and morph over time. Most of us undergo a multiplicity of educational, work, and dating experiences.

Those who marry and raise children experience additional changes. Take a look at wedding photos of any couple who has been married for more than ten years, and ask if they're as close now as they were then to the people in their wedding party. Very few couples can say yes to that.

As a young adult your best friends from college or church seem as crucial to your life as food, water, and your cell phone. But the factors that bind you together fluctuate over time. (A word of advice: if you're torn between having your sister or your best friend serve as your bridesmaid, either have both or choose your sister. You'll probably still be running into her at family gatherings thirty years from now, and you can reminisce.)

The wisdom of growing older will increasingly show us that the manner in which we relate to particular people often needs to change over time.

I thoroughly enjoyed my high school and college days and made plenty of friends. After my wedding I left my hometown and didn't return for several years. All my family had moved away, so it didn't feel like home anymore. When I did finally visit, I met with some old high school friends. We recalled the crazy antics we'd pulled off as youth. We laughed and joked and stretched the truth.

But as enjoyable as it was to recall our frolicking youth, we all knew that time in our lives had passed. As delightful as it had been to swipe toilet paper from the local gas station to wrap the trees in a friend's front yard, we knew that now, as mature adults, we wouldn't be doing *that* anymore (unless of course, someone *really* deserved it).

THIS CAN BE PAINFUL

One of the most painful experiences is when a friendship that once was meaningful and close comes to an end.

Perhaps she was a wild and crazy high school friend who kept you laughing through chemistry class—but with whom you have little in common now that you are in college.

Or you may have had a close friend during your years as a parent of preschoolers, often taking your kids to the park together and having regular combined family get-togethers at each other's homes. But now your kids are teenagers with little in common, and you've moved to different neighborhoods. The aspects of your lives that drew your families together no longer exist.

Or perhaps you had a great friend and colleague at work. You often ate lunch together or carpooled to the office. But you've moved on to another company, and the commonality you shared has dissipated.

Some people feel deep remorse and pain over the loss of a friendship. Clearly, if the dissolution of a relationship is because you were a jerk, you *should* feel regret! But friendships often shift or end simply because one or both friends have entered a winter season in which a stage of life is ending. You do not (or should not) *use* friends and trade them in like amusement park tokens. They may, however, share only a portion of your life's journey.

Much like the man Christian in John Bunyan's classic *The Pilgrim's Progress,* we find ourselves with a variety of companions along life's journey. Those we consider friends have a particular role to play during certain stages of life. Then, as we reach a new milestone in our pilgrimage, some of our traveling companions take the off-ramp and proceed in different directions, while others merge into the lane next to us and join us for the next leg of our trip.

It's all a part of a process that can be as natural as, well, the changing of seasons.

REFLECT AND RESPOND

1. Is it difficult for you to think of bringing a relationship to an end? If so, why is this?

2. How can ending certain relationships offer us freedom and greater capacity for developing new relationships and growing as persons? Do you presently have a relationship that may be holding you back from what God intends for you?

3. Do you carry any guilt for a relationship that has come to an end? Should you?

4. Do you know of someone close to you who is undergoing a winter season at this time? How can you encourage this person with something you've learned so far from this book?

24

OUR ROLES IN WINTER

I spent thirteen enjoyable years as a seminary president. That assignment allowed me to work with brilliant professors, a dedicated staff, talented students, and a highly supportive board of trustees. During those years I began writing books and speaking at conferences around the world, activities that brought me additional gratification. My family loved our life in those days as well. We had a great home and a wonderful church. With all those positive factors surrounding me, the seminary seemed like the perfect place for me to work until I retired.

Then one day I realized I must go. Everything at the school was going well, but after thirteen years I was no longer growing in my job. (I've been told that after ten years most leaders have already made their greatest contributions to their organization.) Sure, I could remain for another twenty years until retirement, but I would merely be *earning* a living, not *living*.

What was actually stretching and growing me was the writing and speaking I was doing. However, it was difficult to develop in that area while I simultaneously carried the responsibility of leading a school. That role in my life needed to end so I would be free to embrace a new stage in life.

It wasn't about money. I ended up taking a pay cut to change jobs. For me at that point, changing roles was about *thriving*. I also realized that, despite all I'd accomplished for the school, it too would benefit from a new leader with fresh ideas and energy.

LETTING GO

Scripture is filled with discussions about dying and what it represents and symbolizes. As a notable example, Jesus said, "Unless a grain of wheat falls into the ground and dies, it remains alone; but if it dies, it produces much grain" (John 12:24). Our natural tendency is to hold on to what we have—whether it's possessions, positions, or people. But Scripture teaches that true living comes from letting go of what we have.

The history of politics provides numerous examples of people who wouldn't let go of their roles. Ulysses S. Grant and Theodore Roosevelt were two of America's most popular presidents while in office. (Grant served for eight years shortly after the Civil War and Roosevelt for seven and a half at the beginning of the twentieth century.) Upon leaving the presidency, both men embarked on world tours. They seemed at first to be transitioning well into their next season in life.

But after just one term away, neither man could refrain from attempting to return to the White House. Both were defeated. Grant gave up after failing to secure enough votes at his party's 1876 nominating convention. Roosevelt came up short at the convention of 1912 but went on to aggressively pursue a national third-party effort, which also proved unsuccessful. Rather than celebrating their presidential contributions and then embracing the next stage of life, these men grasped once again for their former office.

For Roosevelt, this pursuit lost him many friends and proved disastrous for his Republican Party. And it need not have happened, even according to his own values and principles. Midway through his first term as president, while eulogizing one of his cabinet members who had died in office, Roosevelt had written these words:

It is a good thing to die in the harness at the zenith of one's fame, with the consciousness of having lived a long, honorable, and useful life. After we're dead it will not make the slightest difference whether men speak well or ill of us. But in the days and hours before dying, it must be pleasant to feel that you've done your part as a man and have not yet been thrown aside as useless, and that your children and children's children, in short all those that are dearest to you, have just cause for pride in your actions.[29]

If Roosevelt had died during the last week of his presidency, those words would have described his own experience. But he, like Grant, could not leave well enough alone.

This same trap often snares aging sports stars. They were the best in the world, but they continue suiting up long after their most productive days are behind them. While still expecting to be paid top dollar, they now make subpar contributions.

Business executives who were once the wunderkinds of the marketplace watch their companies decline, yet they're often unwilling or unable to step aside and allow younger executives with fresh ideas and modern skills to take the helm. As Oswald Sanders noted, "Advance is held up for years by well-meaning but aging men who refuse to vacate office and insist on holding the reins in their failing hands."[30]

This refusal to acknowledge the winter season of one's life occurs in every level of human endeavor. The office worker who has held the same post for twenty years refuses to retire despite the fact that his skills are archaic. The politician desperately clings to office even though it's clear that winds of change are blowing. The former star quarterback resents the understudies who are nipping at his heels.

Winter is particularly difficult because it follows autumn, when we're at our peak. We're often haunted by thoughts that perhaps we can regain our old form, our former zeal, our previous success. So rather than boldly advancing to the next stage of life, we tenaciously cling to what we know and thereby become stale and stunted in our outdated roles.

Indeed, for some, there comes a time when they must be forcibly removed.

CLINGING TOO LONG

King Hezekiah is a biblical example of someone who clung too long to his God-appointed role. He'd been one of Judah's most righteous and effective monarchs, earning tributes like these: "He trusted in the LORD God of Israel, so that after him was none like him among all the kings of Judah, nor who were before him.... The LORD was with him; he prospered wherever he went" (2 Kings 18:5, 7).

But one day in his later years when Hezekiah had become ill, the esteemed prophet Isaiah informed him in no uncertain terms that winter was setting in on his life and reign: "Thus says the LORD: 'Set your house in order, for you shall die and not live'" (Isaiah 38:1). Rather than once again trusting God and assuming that a new spring was dawning, Hezekiah desperately recoiled from death, weeping bitterly (verses 2–3).

God responded in mercy, graciously agreeing to extend the king's life span by fifteen years. Hezekiah was delighted, but his nation suffered grievously. During this added period of Hezekiah's reign, his son Manasseh was born—a man destined to succeed Hezekiah and to become the most evil and ungodly king ever to rule the nation. Furthermore, the aging king naively revealed to Babylonian envoys his extensive royal treasure (Isaiah 39), and the ambassadors took note of it. The Babylonian army later returned to Jerusalem, relieved it of the royal treasure, and utterly destroyed the city in the process. Had Hezekiah accepted the winter season in his life, his descendants might have avoided horrific suffering.

A plethora of signs can indicate to us that winter has arrived in one of our current roles. Our skills may no longer be adequate. Our successes are all in the past, with no fresh victories occurring. We may no longer have a sense of direction for the future. We may have lost our passion for our work. Colleagues may no longer be as supportive of us as they once were. The boss may not be as encouraging or as appreciative of our efforts. Our focus and passion may have moved on to other activities and interests.

Many people are earning the most money or experiencing their greatest success when winter strikes, so we may find it hard to walk away even if our hearts are urging us to do so. We may think, *Well I'll remain one more year... I'll wait until I'm retirement age... I'll hold on until my son is out of college...* It's far better to nobly walk away from a current role and to embrace the next spring season of life than to stubbornly remain entrenched until people resent us or remove us.

SADNESS AND FEAR

Even good things come to an end. Unfortunately, we may view winter as an ominous season and instinctively recoil, allowing ourselves to be dominated by feelings of sadness and fear.

We feel *sadness* because we recognize that an important stage of life is over. Whether it's our carefree preschool days, our vigorous high school years, our time of parenting young children, or our working career, it's natural to be sad when leaving activities we've enjoyed. It's fine to shed a few tears at our company's farewell party or as we drop our "baby" off at her college dormitory, but we eventually must regain our composure and enter the new spring of life, anticipating fresh opportunities on the horizon.

Fear is the second feeling we confront in winter. Sometimes we reluctantly experience closure before a new door opens. We get laid off at work due to downsizing or a corporate merger. We recognize a new stage of life is emerging, but hope for the future doesn't exactly pay the bills. What will the new job be? Or we retire from our career before knowing what we'll do next. Or we send our last child off to college without having any idea what we'll do with an empty nest.

Every time we see one stage of life draw to a close, we may feel apprehensive about what is coming. But we must not allow fear to drive us to cling to a bygone role and to resent those who suggest (or insist) that we move on.

For with God, there's always another role to undertake, a fresh assignment, and another task that will call upon everything we've experienced and learned thus far. God is never finished with us. He may, however, be finished with our current role. If so, we must be prepared to take on the next assignment that inevitably comes.

REFLECT AND RESPOND

1. Of all the most important roles in your life, in which ones, if any, are you now experiencing a winter season, a time of winding down to a close?

2. Looking at your past, what lessons have you learned when certain roles in your life came to an end?

3. What do you think are the most important signs to watch for, indicating that it's time to let go of a certain role in your life? What can help you be more alert to these?

4. Do you have a current role that you are holding on to when you should be letting it go? If you do, why are you unwilling to walk away from it?

5. Are you bitter about roles you lost or were removed from in the past? Should you be? Could it be that you didn't recognize a winter season in your life?

25

WINTER AND OUR FAITH

A final area of our lives that's deeply impacted by winter is our faith.

There are periods in life when we reach the end of a road in our faith journey. At this point we've initiated new understandings of God during spring, developed those dimensions to our faith in summer, then finally achieved maturity in autumn. Ultimately we reach winter—the culmination of many dimensions to our spiritual life.

Three of the most important aspects to our winter faith are *celebration, blessing,* and *rest.*

CELEBRATION

Winter is the final season in the seasonal cycle. And when you get to the end…you need to celebrate!

Last year I participated in a tour of Israel, joining my parents, my brother and sister-in-law, and my son Mike. Israel has so many amazing places to see! One site I particularly wanted to visit was Masada, a massive, isolated fortress built atop a mountain beside the Dead Sea. A generation after the time of Christ, in the Great Revolt of the Jews against Rome, Masada was the scene of the final showdown between Jewish zealots and Roman forces. In the autumn of AD 72, Lucius Flavius Silva led the Tenth Roman Legion against Masada, the final Jewish stronghold.

Inside it nearly a thousand Jewish zealots vainly hoped for deliverance. After a siege of several months, the Romans breached the walls on April 16—only to discover the inhabitants had chosen to commit mass suicide rather than be enslaved.

As someone who loves history, I found this story fascinating. (Even my sons find history interesting as long as there has been a battle, a castle, or a dragon.) However, what I found particularly taxing in visiting this site was the Snake Path, which winds its way from the mountaintop fortress to the ground far below. On my first visit there two years earlier, my sons—both in their early twenties at the time—challenged me to walk down the path with them. It mattered not to them that the temperature was 100 degrees that day or that there was an air-conditioned cable car fully prepared to glide us gently down to the bottom. The contest was on.

The first leg of our descent appeared charming enough. I shot out of the gate at a brisk pace, catching a spectacular view of the Dead Sea to the east. I hoped to make serious progress before the first bead of sweat emerged on my brow and my body began to grow weary. I had, of course, scoffed at the idea of bringing a water bottle, not wanting to add unnecessary weight to my load.

I had one delay as I ended up behind a couple who were walking slowly down the middle of the narrow pathway, preventing anyone from passing. I thought if I used a reliable North American technique and "rode their tail," they would grow weary of having me breathing (heavily by that time) down their neck. When they finally stepped aside, I smugly maneuvered past them until I noticed that the man was an off-duty Israeli soldier with a machine gun hanging at his waist. (I'm grateful my Type A personality didn't incite an international incident!)

Two-thirds of the way down, my mouth was parched. Visions of iced coffee machines were dancing before my bleary eyes. My legs were throbbing and in danger of buckling. I had to will my feet to take each step.

Finally reaching the bottom, I staggered into the gift shop, where my mother saw me. She was so distressed at the sight of me that she grabbed a water bottle from another tourist's hands and insisted that I drink it immediately.

That had been my first trip to Masada. This year we returned, and this time my son declared that *descending* the Snake Path was for women and children; *ascending* the Snake Path is what separated the men from the boys.

This time I took a water bottle with me, which I emptied before we made the first turn in the path. Then I began to frantically discard cheaper souvenirs from my pockets in an effort to lighten my load.

By the time I was halfway up, my legs were shaking so much you would have thought my ascent had been choreographed by *High School Musical*. I don't know what I would have done had it not been for the support I received from my son—as when he encouraged me to step to the side so some elderly women could pass. But I made it!

And what a celebration at the top! Getting there had been difficult, but then, significant accomplishments usually are.

Winter is the time to catch our breath, remember, and celebrate what has come to an end.

From a perspective of faith, we recognize that each stage of life is a divine gift. I'm reminded of the sage words of George Burns, who said, "If you live to be a hundred, you've got it made. Very few people die past that age."

The fact is, every time we reach a milestone in our lives, it calls for celebration.

BLESSING

A second important aspect of winter is our ability and willingness to *bless others*. If we view the seasons of our lives as God's gift to us, then we'll readily bless those who follow. We may be in winter ourselves, but we can place our lives next to those who are excitedly entering spring or laboring in summer or harvesting in autumn.

Scripture urges us, "Let your speech always be with grace" (Colossians 4:6); we're told to render blessing to each other (even to the undeserving), "knowing that you were called to this" (1 Peter 3:9). God wants to use our words to bless!

But sadly, people in winter often are too preoccupied with their own issues to take time to encourage those coming behind them. We shouldn't become so busy grieving over what is ending in our lives that we neglect the opportunity in words and in actions to inspire those who are entering the stage we're vacating.

I recall a time when our sons were preschoolers. I was a student, and we lived in a small apartment. Money was scarce, so we rarely ate out. It was a *huge* event for our kids when we did venture into a "real" restaurant (one without a red-haired clown and a PlayPlace).

On one of those outings, our boys giggled and laughed throughout the meal and, of course, dropped the occasional food particle on the floor. For them it was a grand adventure. Every time they burst into laughter, Lisa and I were paranoid that customers would sign a petition to have our uncivilized family forcibly removed from the premises.

I noticed an older couple occasionally glancing our way. They clearly were empty nesters and probably annoyed they had to endure preschoolers on their date night.

As they got up to leave, I noticed they were approaching our table. *Oh no, here it comes.* I mentally began preparing a rebuttal: *There must have been an unusually high sugar content in my children's chicken strips,* or maybe, *Normally they don't act so barbaric, but their naps got cut short today due to a solar eclipse.*

But to our surprise they said, "We wanted to come and tell you how much we enjoyed watching your little boys having such a good time!" Wow! Of all the comments I anticipated, that wasn't one of them!

That couple blessed us. They'd been down that road. They knew how desperate young couples are to escape their home and exhausting routine. Rather than being grumpy winter critics, they chose to uplift a young couple working hard in summer to raise their children. More than twenty years later I obviously still remember that thoughtful gesture, and I've found myself looking for situations to do the same.

If, as a senior in high school, you're the captain of your football team, you can either grieve the fact this is your last year to play competitive football, or you can spend time encouraging the rookies on the team, knowing they'll assume the mantle of leadership after you're gone. Likewise, if your children grow up and move out of the house, you can complain that they never call or visit, or you can encourage them as they build their adult lives in their own homes.

As we exit each stage of life, we have the choice to go kicking and screaming or blessing and encouraging. I think you know which of those responses people want most from you!

Winter can also bring a sense of urgency to mend neglected or broken relationships and to complete unfinished business. This is an important aspect of working through the winter season, and it takes time and effort. Some people move from one stage of life to the next, leaving a trail of broken relationships and hurt feelings in their wake. I've known people who injured so many people in one stage of life that they were anxious to move on to the next stage with a fresh start at unencumbered relationships. Parents were only too glad to cart their teen off to college so the shouting matches at home could end. Employees left their workplaces with colleagues throwing their farewell party *after* they left.

Would you agree that the way we leave one stage of life greatly affects how we enter the next? When the apostle Paul was writing to believers in Thessalonica, he recalled, "For you remember, brethren, our labor and toil; for laboring night and day, that we might not be a burden to any of you, we preached to you the gospel of God. You are witnesses, and God also, how devoutly and justly and blamelessly we behaved ourselves among you who believe" (1 Thessalonians 2:9–10). Paul didn't leave loose ends. When he walked away from a stage of his life, he left nothing undone, and people grieved to see him go.

REST

The last area that's particularly important in winter is *rest*. In farming terms, winter is when fields lie dormant and we live off the stored harvest. (And if you had a *really* successful harvest, you rest on a beach in Florida!)

God could have created nature to have a perpetual growing season. But He knew that the land and its occupants needed down time. Isn't it interesting that Scripture indicates that God, after creating for six days, rested on the seventh (Genesis 2:1–3)? Obviously He didn't need to restore His strength, but He rested anyway. It's the pattern God established for His creatures.

Resting helps us rejuvenate before launching into a new season. It's crucial that we allow certain stages of our lives to properly come to an end. I've known people who, having lost their jobs, became so anxious to find their next employment that they were filled with worry. Yet God provided for their needs, right on schedule. These people often confess later that they regret not *resting* before they hurried into their next job. The human body wasn't designed (physically or emotionally) to go hard all the time.

This may be one reason that winter is an underutilized season. People dread endings, and they fear idleness, so they miss the God-orchestrated opportunity to rest. As a result, some people race from one role to the next. They embrace each stage of life with gusto, but little time is given to restoration or reflection.

Winter is when we need to benefit from the mental clarity that comes with rest and relaxation and ask ourselves questions like these:

What have I learned from this stage of life?

How might I have enjoyed a more productive autumn?

Did I bring important aspects of my life to their proper end?

Do I want my next spring to be different from my last?

Some people never slow down, even in winter, so they undergo identical experiences over and over again.

Winter provides the opportunity to step back from our labors and to reflect, celebrate, and adjust. Some people do this, and they advance through life as increasingly wiser and contented human beings. Others fail to do this. Consequently, they exist and work, but they don't *thrive*.

TAKING TIME TO GIVE

Andrew Mellon was one of the most successful businesspeople of the early twentieth century. By the time of his death in 1937, he was one of the wealthiest people in America. He'd invested profitably in banking, oil, and aluminum and also served as a popular secretary of the treasury for eleven years, under three presidents. He bequeathed a fortune in paintings and helped to found the National Gallery of Art in Washington DC.

Yet his extremely driven nature prevented him from employing the winters of his life to reflect, to learn, and to change. Mellon's biographer makes this observation:

> Where Andrew failed to equal, let alone surpass, his father [Judge Thomas Mellon] was in the range and richness of his humanity. Behind the Judge's implacably stern façade was a warmhearted and emotional spirit, moved by the tragedy and transience of life. Yet behind Andrew's no less steely exterior, it often seemed to many people, and especially now to Nora [Andrew Mellon's wife], that there was either something vaguely unpleasant—or nothing at all. He was a hollow man, with no interior life. He could judge men and business, but not women and love.[31]

Whereas tycoons such as John D. Rockefeller transferred their wealth to their heirs during their lifetime, Mellon seemed to need every moment of his long life to complete his enormous workload. By the time he was seventy-eight, Rockefeller had given away $275 million to charity and $35 million to his children. In the next five years, he gave an additional $200 million to charity and $475 million to his children (leaving himself a paltry $25 million to scrape by on until he died shortly before his ninety-eighth birthday).[32]

On the other hand, as Mellon neared the close of his life, his only son asked him for two paintings that he'd grown up with in his childhood home. Mellon offered to sell them to his son for $25,000 apiece.[33] Mellon did ultimately donate a vast sum to the National Gallery of Art, but he never took time in the winter of his days to fully reflect on what was most important in life. As a result, he missed out on much of the joy that could have been his.

EMBRACING DEATH

Perhaps the most ominous aspect of rest in winter comes at death. For those without faith in the divine, death promises little other than, perhaps, an absence of further suffering. But to those who trust that the afterlife provides delights unimaginable on earth, death is but the final winter before an everlasting spring.

Janice Hudson was an emergency flight nurse in San Francisco for more than ten years, and in her career she daily cared for people in serious physical distress. After helping save hundreds of people and seeing others die, she came to these conclusions:

> There is a certain lovely rhythm in life; as the Bible says, a time to be born, and a time to die.... Most laypeople view death as inevitably tragic. I feel, quite to the contrary, that death is a natural part of life. It's the circumstances that can be tragic. I've spent time with elderly patients who know their death is approaching, and many look forward to being released from bodies that have been ravaged by time and disease. I was initially afraid of this aspect of nursing, and found myself being comforted by the very

people I was supposedly caring for. From these people I've
learned that death is often a peaceful process that can be
likened to rebirth.[34]

Hudson goes on to note that some people will desperately fight
impending death, futilely spending hundreds of thousands of dollars on
medical expenses in a desperate attempt to delay the inevitable.

Contrast this to the way the apostle Paul approached his demise.
"For me," he affirmed, "to live is Christ, and to die is gain. But if I live on
in the flesh, this will mean fruit from my labor; yet what I shall choose I
cannot tell. For I am hard-pressed between the two, having a desire to
depart and be with Christ, which is far better" (Philippians 1:21–23).
Clearly, Paul saw himself in a win-win situation. In this life he served the
Lord and blessed as many people as he could. But when his earthly days
were finished, he was eager to enter a world of indescribable heavenly
rapture.

Such a view of life and death enables us to live with fervency but then
to accept death with resolve and dignity because we have an inkling of
what awaits us on the other side.

MOVING FORWARD

Winter has unique qualities that we must embrace if we're to experience
full lives. It offers a time of withdrawal, rest, and closure.

Nothing on earth is meant to last forever…including *us*. If we trust
in divine providence, then we don't need to fear winter, because we know
there'll always be another spring. To cling to our present lives during
winter demonstrates a profound lack of faith. We're meant to thrive in
each stage of life and then, when winter sets in, to set that stage of life
aside and enthusiastically embrace the next one.

This is how your life is supposed to be lived: in seasons. And every
cycle of those seasons will include a time of winter.

REFLECT AND RESPOND

1. This chapter emphasized three dimensions of winter faith—celebration, blessing others, and rest. Which of these do you do best? Which is most difficult for you?

2. What have you learned in winter as you reflected and rested?

3. Do you struggle with resting? Have you been working continually without using the winter seasons of your life to be restored?

4. What is your view of death? Are you prepared for it? Do you fear it? Why?

5. In your own experience, what is it about winter seasons that especially requires your trust in God?

PART THREE

THRIVING *in* ALL OUR SEASONS

26

HOLDING OUR SEASONS TOGETHER

My hope for you as you've been reading this book is that you'll become more aware and better motivated to *thrive* in every season—to truly get the most out of every moment in the one precious, nontransferable life you have.

If you're like me, that doesn't come naturally.

NOT IN THE MOOD

I was exhausted. I had a right to be. I'd traveled across the country that week, speaking in three different cities. And after crossing two time zones, enduring a grumpy TSA agent, and languishing beside an agonizingly slow luggage carousel, I finally pulled into my garage a little past midnight early Sunday morning.

As I entered my house, my thinking was gnarled in tension. In only a few hours I was supposed to go to church. *However,* I'd spoken eight times that week in three different Christian-oriented conferences. I'd also listened to sermons and devotionals from a wide array of outstanding speakers. And after all, wasn't I jet-lagged? and road weary? And hadn't I personally preached *eight* sermons last week? *Surely I could be excused for getting some badly needed sleep and missing church just this once!*

But I had a serious problem. There were three teenagers living under my roof (all of whom were close relatives—*very* close). It would be mortifying if they dutifully marched off to church while their dad remained behind, slumbering in bed.

So when morning's light dawned oh so soon, I willed myself out from under my thick comforter and did my duty.

I can't say I was enamored with the process. In fact, it was a lot like eating oatmeal; you do it because it's the right thing to do. Have you ever gone to church for that reason and that reason alone?

To exacerbate my problem, the worship leader that morning chose again to have the congregation sing a favorite chorus of his that I was particularly unfond of (okay, I despised it). Mind you, the tune was catchy enough, and there were a few good lyrics embedded deeply within it. My conundrum was that there were also some *awful* phrases that I couldn't bring myself to sing because I deemed them not only scandalously self-centered but also blatantly untrue. I refuse to say things in church I believe are false (even if they're put to music). So normally whenever we sang this chorus, I would sing the parts I felt were theologically correct, but then I'd cough or suddenly look heavenward (as if struck with a sublime inspiration) until the offensive lyrics had passed.

But that particular morning I didn't have it in me to pretend. So I grimly folded my arms (I don't normally do this—honest!) and determined to wait out the disturbing song.

To kill time, I gazed around the auditorium to see what the naive victims around me were doing. I noticed both my teenage sons on the platform, enthusiastically playing instruments on the worship team. I began to feel uneasy.

I glanced down the row to my daughter. She was singing her heart out, praising God. (Was it hot in there, or was it just me?)

It was then that I heard the still, small voice: "Do you ever want your kids to look over at their dad in a worship service and see him *frowning*?"

My mind raced back to a lunch I'd had several years earlier. The special guest was a man from China who'd spent fifteen years in prison, much of it in solitary confinement, because he was a pastor. During our meal I'd asked the man a question: How had he spent his Sundays in solitary confinement? That now seems like a silly question. But I'll never forget his answer. He described how he would worship God, all alone, on that cold, concrete floor in that cramped, foul-smelling cell. As he sang and prayed, there were times when God's presence would palpably fill his cell until the pastor was overwhelmed by God's goodness.

That was the memory I recalled as I stood, arms folded, impatiently awaiting the conclusion of the annoying song.

God has a way of speaking in a quiet, gentle manner that's deafening. He simply asked, *Is this all it takes for you to feel unable to worship Me? After all I've done for you, you can't find any reason at this moment to praise and thank Me?*

I stood convicted. I live in a country where I'm free to worship God anytime I choose without fear of reprisals or being carted off to prison. I can haul a wheelbarrow load of Bibles and Christian publications into church with me if I wish. My chair that day was comfortable, the room temperature perfect, the worship service carefully planned and professionally executed, and, most of all, God was fully present. Yet I'd chosen to be miserable.

Right there I made a commitment that every time I have an opportunity to worship God and enjoy His presence, I'm going to do so, with gusto. I don't care if the only accompaniment is a palsied, tone-deaf bagpipe player; if there's an opportunity to let God know how grateful I am for what He has done for me, I'm going to do it!

Now, there's something else you should know about this: *I can't sing.* But I view that as a minor detail.

The other day my daughter, Carrie, went with me to a local church where I was to speak. During the song service she kept looking at me with a pained expression. I finally whispered to her, "Are you okay? Do you *need* something?"

She responded, "Are you doing that on purpose?"

"Doing what?" I asked.

"Singing off key on every note! I've heard people miss an occasional high note or a very low note," she said, "but I didn't think it was possible to miss every one!"

Let's just say my singing has attracted some quizzical looks in church services. People sitting in front of me have become suddenly alarmed that a Canadian bull moose has inadvertently wandered into the church foyer and is mournfully bellowing for its mate. But that's okay. I'm not singing for them anyway.

THRIVING IN EVERY SITUATION

I learned something extremely important during that worship service. I found that you can remove my favorite music, and I can still worship freely and fully. You can abscond with my church, health, money, and even my freedom, and it's still possible for me not only to survive but thrive. How so? It's because of an incredible truth.

Imagine you're in heaven. Towering before you is the enormous glittering throne of almighty God. Myriads of angels continually cry out a thundering chorus of "Holy! Holy! Holy!" Saints from ages past lie prostrate before His awesome throne. Despite all the times you read your Bible during your earthly sojourn and dreamed of this moment, the reality of God's presence absolutely overwhelms you. It's so beyond anything you imagined.

Now ask yourself: What would you be sensing? Awe? Terror? Love? Peace?

Here's something I know you would feel: joy! (You'll undoubtedly experience those other emotions too.) As David wrote, "In Your presence is fullness of joy; at Your right hand are pleasures forevermore" (Psalm 16:11).

That may not be what you were taught in church. You may have been informed that drawing near to God is serious and somber business, that frowns are standard fare as you ponder deep and important doctrines and are riddled with guilt over your numerous sins. But the Bible indicates that in God's presence you'll experience perfect, undiluted joy.

Recall again those words in John 15 about Jesus as the vine and us as fruitful branches. Jesus described the Christian life as "abiding" in Him and explained that believers should live in the same intimate communion with Christ as a branch enjoys with a vine. Remember that Jesus concluded by saying, "These things I have spoken to you, that My joy may remain in you, and that your joy may be full" (verse 11). Jesus was affirming what David had said: when you're close to God, you experience joy.

A caveat is in order here. The joy of the Lord isn't identical to what the world calls "happiness." You can become happy at the drop of a hat. You inherit a fortune from an uncle you didn't even know you had, your favorite team wins the title (or in my case, scrapes into the playoffs), you get a raise, someone says they like your new outfit, the sun is shining, you find a parking space by the front door of your office building, the traffic cop lets you off with a warning, the dentist says you have no cavities... Happiness arises from a multitude of sources. It stems from your physical appetites or mental and emotional expectations being met so that you experience some form of pleasure.

The next time you're at a magazine stand, peruse a mag that chronicles the lives of Hollywood stars. Such tabloids exult in the means by which the world produces happiness. Conversely, the same conditions that make happiness relatively easy to obtain can likewise cause it to quickly dissolve: your dentist informs you that the pain in your jaw can be alleviated with a root canal; you're passed over for a promotion; it's a cloudy day; traffic is horrible; you didn't sleep a wink last night; your team loses; you're diagnosed with a serious illness.

What makes the joy of the Lord so invaluable is that it stems not from the world but from God's presence. That's why unbelievers can experience happiness but not divine joy.

The source and substance of this heavenly joy bring an important consequence. *No one* and *nothing* can rob you of it! On the eve of Jesus's arrest and crucifixion, He promised His disciples that their joy was something "no one will take from you" (John 16:22).

Now, you may be thinking, "That can't be true. I lose my joy all the time!" But notice that Jesus didn't say you couldn't *lose* your joy; He stated that no one could *take* it from you. Since true joy comes from God's presence, no one can remove Him from you. Of course, you can *surrender* your joy any time you decide that your boss or wayward child or unemployment or spouse or arthritis is too much even for God's presence to overcome. But that's your choice.

When you're enjoying God's presence, even persecution or job loss or terminal disease cannot suppress your joy. That's what my Chinese pastor friend discovered. The government robbed him of his job, family, friends, reputation, money, and freedom, but they could not remove God's presence. So, alone in a cold, damp prison cell, he could bask in the joy of divine companionship.

Paul and Silas experienced the same thing. They were slandered, publicly humiliated, beaten, and imprisoned by evil men for a crime they didn't commit, yet at midnight they sang hymns of praise to God (Acts 16:16–25). It seems incredible that after all they had endured those men could still be thanking God for His goodness. But they were. They had learned to enjoy God's presence even when their feet were shackled in painful stocks inside a dungeon. To them God was not merely a doctrine to believe; He was a Person to enjoy.

Charles Spurgeon summed up our situation well:

To know that Jesus loves me is one thing, but to be visited by Him in love is much more....

It is a pity that we know so much about Christ and yet enjoy Him so little. Our experience ought to keep pace with our knowledge.[35]

WHAT HOLDS ALL OUR SEASONS TOGETHER?

Why is this question important as it relates to the stages of our lives?

It's because, as we've seen, life is full of changes. Seasons come and go. The stages of life can dramatically alter our circumstances. Our closest relationships can enter winter seasons. We'll inevitably experience loss and hardship. But what's the glue that holds our lives together? What's the one constant reality throughout life that never changes?

God.

He's the God who said, "I am the LORD, *I do not change;* therefore you are not consumed" (Malachi 3:6). He's the God "with whom there is *no variation or shadow of turning*" (James 1:17).

What makes life's changing seasons work so beautifully is that there's one consistent reality throughout our earthly pilgrimage: *God's presence.* He ties together every loose end and diverse experience to produce a life that's meaningful, joyful, and abundant.

And what's even more amazing is that God does far more than merely hold your life together; He enables you to flourish. The closer you walk with Him, the more of Him you experience.

Unfortunately, what most of us have witnessed, especially in North America, is many people who claim to be Christians and yet appear joyless. They may go to church every week, but they seldom have a smile on their faces.

As an itinerant speaker I've visited numerous churches around the world. It has puzzled me to watch longtime saints sitting glumly in their pews while the congregation sings about God's amazing grace or about how great the Father's love for them is. At times I've wondered if I'd inadvertently entered the Sacred Church of the Sour Lemons. It's almost as

if wraithlike ushers accosted each person at the door and compelled them
to chew a lemon rind before entering the sanctuary.

But that's not the way God intends for His people to live and certainly not how He wants to be worshiped. Too often there's a noticeable
disconnect between what we claim to believe about God and the way we
live.

It takes our concerted, intentional effort to cut loose from this tendency that drags many of us into an existence far beneath what God
intends for us. So I want to focus next on a few key practices and attitudes
that will enable you to thrive—joyfully—in every season of your life.

REFLECT AND RESPOND

1. Are you a joyful person? Where would you rate yourself on
   a scale of one to ten?

2. Would you describe your current life as thriving? Why or
   why not?

3. Describe what thriving in life would look like to you. What
   would be happening in your life if you were truly thriving?

4. What's the difference between having fun and experiencing
   joy? How do they overlap?

5. In what area of life do you find it most difficult to thrive
   and to experience joy? What could help you most to press
   through to a fuller experience of joy in this area?

27

THREE KEYS

As we've discussed seasons and how they affect us, we've seen how important it is to stay alert to what's happening to us throughout life's stages. Such recognition is fundamental to knowing how to get the most out of each season.

But there's more to thriving in life than self-awareness. Let me share three overarching factors that can dramatically enhance the quality of your life, season by season.

A CONSCIOUS AIM

We've talked about *thriving, not just surviving*—something that needs to become more than a mere slogan for us. Let me urge you to make this your conscious, deliberate intention.

I'm on an airplane almost every week, and to make traveling slightly more bearable, I have a membership in an airport lounge. But I'm not sure it relieves much stress. That's because many people assume they must shout into their cell phones to be heard. Or perhaps they assume everyone on the premises *wants* to hear them trying to make a deal with a skeptical buyer, or rudely berating their hapless administrative assistant, or getting caught up with their kids back home while vainly promising to spend more time together upon their return. I'd almost swear some people in those lounges systematically call every person in their contact list in a vain effort to alleviate their loneliness.

In those lounges, as well as in airport corridors and on the planes themselves, you can't help but overhear a *lot* of conversations. And they've led me to believe that people in the business community tend to be over-the-top stressed. I've even seen them exit airplanes while simultaneously conducting conversations on two cell phones. They're often unhappy people who no doubt make those they interact with unhappy as well. They can boast to total strangers about returns on their investments while their personal relationships are clearly in shambles.

Unfortunately this affliction strikes more than the business set. Too many people, even self-professing Christians, are trying to get by *without experiencing real joy.*

During a flight to Hong Kong, I sat next to an airline pilot who was on a break. In his spare time he'd formed a leadership development company that analyzed airline disasters and then used the lessons learned to teach leadership skills. I listened to his insights into why well-trained pilots in state-of-the-art aircraft had flown into mountains or run out of fuel, causing huge loss of life. From a logical, twenty-twenty hindsight perspective, the flight crew's mistakes appeared obvious.

Then this man mentioned that in the following month he would be getting married for the second time. I couldn't help but ask (I think it was my mother coming out in me) if he'd applied the same analytical skills that he used to dissect airline disasters to determine why his first marriage ultimately failed. He seemed surprised but intrigued at my question.

I suggested that perhaps he was a Type A personality who held down two demanding jobs and expected to be unquestioningly obeyed by his subordinates. I asked if his first wife had been classified as a subordinate and had eventually rebelled against his management style. He admitted she had.

"What adjustments have you made," I then asked, "so that your second marriage doesn't end up crashing like your first?"

He hadn't made any. This guy seemed like a nice person with above-average intelligence. Yet he was charging through life and experiencing some catastrophic failures along the way. He could detect the mistakes others made, but he'd failed to carefully evaluate his own life and priorities so he could achieve a truly contented life.

I gave him my card but never heard from him. I've often wondered if his second marriage lasted.

The bottom line is this: life is too precious merely to get by or to charge through without making course corrections. God designed you to thrive. Don't settle for less.

Remember that *you*—not your parents or boss or church or children—are responsible for your life. Whether you thrive in the one life you'll ever have depends solely upon you.

Don't let anything—whether past decisions and behaviors or present limitations—rob you of your joy today. You can experience abundant life in every season.

When former president George H. W. Bush turned seventy-five, he didn't bemoan the fact he was getting older; he went skydiving! He had so much fun that he also leaped out of a plane on his eightieth and eighty-fifth birthdays.

Recently Fauja Singh of Great Britain completed the Toronto Waterfront Marathon. It took him eight hours, twenty-five minutes, and sixteen seconds—an excellent time, considering he was one hundred years old. Singh took up running eleven years earlier when his wife and son died. Upon becoming the first centenarian to complete a marathon, he claimed he was "overjoyed" and that it was "like getting married again." When asked his secret to his vigor, he replied, "The secret to a long and healthy life is to be stressfree. Be grateful for everything you have, stay away from people who are negative, stay smiling…and keep running."[36]

These people chose to experience everything life had to offer them, no matter what stage of life or season or altitude they were in.

Scripture declares that, ultimately, joy doesn't stem from jumping out of airplanes or running for twenty-six miles. Pure, unquenchable joy results from abiding in God's presence (Psalm 16:11; John 15:11). God promises that if we'll draw near to Him, He'll draw near to us (James 4:8). That's the only path to experiencing divine joy in life.

Life is too brief and too difficult at times to experience it joylessly. The world will try to convince you that it's the person with the most toys or money who wins in life. Not so. It's those who live their lives with the most joy.

Hopefully this book has provided you a fresh perspective on your life. Perhaps it helps explain experiences you've had in the past. I pray it has encouraged you to fully embrace your life *today*. And I hope you're excited about what's coming,

Every person is in a season of life. Each season has a unique purpose and contributes something meaningful to our existence. My heartfelt wish is that you would joyfully live your life to its maximum extent throughout each of the seasons of God.

A FOCUS ON WHERE YOU ARE *NOW*

The second key is your firm commitment to *thrive where you are.*

When Carrie was four, she was enamored with Dorothy from *The Wizard of Oz,* especially her bright red shoes. Carrie pleaded with her mother for a pair of Dorothy's footwear.

Upon receiving them, she eagerly placed them on her feet, squeezed her eyes tightly shut, enthusiastically tapped her heels, and fervently chanted, "There's no place like Disney World! There's no place like Disney World!" Clearly, she had other destinations in mind than Kansas.

Often people fail to thrive because they wish they were somewhere else, in a different season. They're in summer, but they act as if they're in spring. Or winter has come, but they want to hold on to autumn. The key to maximizing your life is to fervently embrace your current season.

One reason there are so many young, unmarried mothers is because young couples are too eager to move on to summer pleasures while prepared only for springtime responsibilities. Or people in the summer season of rearing their children grow to resent the burden they carry and choose to enter a springtime affair.

How about you? Are you in the midst of the summer of your career but wistfully dreaming of winter and your retirement years?

Some people hate their lives. At times their situations may reflect the consequences of their own decisions. Others, unfortunately, experience problems inflicted on them by factors largely beyond their control. Their company is sold, and they're laid off. Their child is born with a disability. A storm or flood demolishes their home. Their father dies in a car accident. Their business partner absconds with company assets and leaves them facing bankruptcy. A girl's boyfriend jilts her and takes up with her (former) best friend. There are numerous random calamities that could blindside us at any moment. But at what point do we surrender our joy? What event causes us to conclude that our lives can no longer be joyful?

In an earlier book I described the "joy threshold."[37] This is the level of pain at which you yield your joy to your circumstances. It's when you conclude, "I cannot have joy when my boss treats me this way… when my turkey dressing is dry… when my nose is stuffed up… when my child is a terror… when my football team loses…"

Everyone has a different threshold. For some it isn't very high. Their team losing by a field goal puts them in a bad mood the remainder of the week (or year). For others, like Paul and Silas, even being beaten within an inch of their lives couldn't remove their joy.

My son Daniel has always been ready to make the best of things. When he was barely old enough to talk, one of his regular sayings was, "I'm just not gonna let it get me down!"

I recall one bedtime when he was a four-year-old. He wouldn't settle down and go to sleep, so I confiscated the toys he had with him in bed. Hearing more noise emanating from his room, I returned and discovered he had a stash of contraband toys hidden in his bed sheets. I systematically stripped his bed bare to ensure he had no more distractions to his slumber. I was about to exit his room when Daniel smiled, held up his pudgy fingers, and said, "That's okay, Daddy. I'll just play with these. You can't take *these* away!" I've learned a lot from Daniel.

The key, of course, is what Brother Lawrence described centuries ago: "practicing the presence of God." It involves living each day and every hour with the conscious awareness of God's active involvement in your life. It's responding to His unfathomable desire to walk with you through every experience.

The apostle Paul described how he learned this truth in 2 Corinthians 12:7–11. No one could accuse this man of being a wimp or a pessimist! But one day Paul reached his limit. He apparently suffered a "thorn in the flesh" that was so grievous he begged God three times to take it away. God didn't. Instead the Lord did something better. He gave Paul His grace and His presence.

Paul had prayed for comfort; God granted him a Comforter.

Which would you rather have—an absence of discomfort or God Himself personally ministering to you and walking with you throughout your pain? God gave Paul *Himself,* and Paul later declared, "Therefore most gladly I will rather boast in my infirmities, that the power of Christ may rest upon me" (verse 9). We have no record of Paul ever asking God to remove that nasty thorn again (although, for the last two millennia, Christians have desperately wanted to know what it was).

So what's the key to thriving in *every* season of life? Choosing to embrace the season and stage of life you're in and walking closely with God through each one. The solution isn't necessarily to change your circumstances but to learn to enjoy God's presence whatever your situation.

I know people who faced painful experiences yet chose joy in the midst of them. One woman's husband walked out on her and filed for divorce. This abandoned wife held on to God and let Him bring her joy in the midst of the most heart-wrenching experience of her life. After eleven years her husband returned, they remarried, and today they lead a ministry to broken marriages.

My brother-in-law had been married a year when he discovered his beautiful young bride had an inoperable brain tumor. That was thirty years ago. Although her health has declined steadily, the two of them have made the best life possible for themselves. In her forties she had to move into a nursing home, and he lives nearby in their house. For every breakfast, lunch, and dinner, the kitchen staff set up a private table for the two of them to eat together and share each other's company. Is it the life they dreamed of as high school sweethearts? Of course not. But rather than deciding that their lives were over while still in their twenties, they've made the best of the life they have.

I have a friend who lost both arms in a tragic accident. Today he lives an active life, has raised a family, and has joy. (He also scared the daylights out of me the first time he drove me through a major city!)

Would these people prefer their lives to be different? Certainly. But were they going to store their joy in the attic with their high school scrapbooks until life miraculously transformed into a fairy tale? No. Life is too precious to waste wishing that things beyond our control would change.

So it is with the seasons of life. We can't determine the severity of spring tornadoes or summer droughts or fall hurricanes or winter blizzards, but we can choose to abide in Christ's presence so that we're filled with His joy, rain or shine.

As you've gone through this book and related what you've read to your own life, you've no doubt identified a particular season you're currently experiencing. Perhaps it's spring, and you're exploring new possibilities. Maybe you're in summer, working hard and developing your skills, knowledge, and experience. You could be in autumn, having reached the pinnacle of your influence and achievement in a certain domain. Or you might be in winter, bringing a stage of your life to a close.

Whatever season you're in, *embrace it fully*. Remember not to rush the process. If you're in spring, investigate your possibilities thoroughly and consciously prepare yourself in ways that seem wise, laying the best foundation in character and commitment for whatever's to come. If you're in summer, don't begrudge its demands, but roll up your sleeves and work hard and effectively. If you're in autumn, strive to produce your best work and to bless others along the way. If you're in winter, don't resist it; allow God to show you how to leave this stage of your life gracefully and with dignity, and be sure to rest and reflect so you're prepared for the coming spring.

Experience your current season fully. The next one will come soon enough!

DOING IT TOGETHER

The third and final key I recommend is your commitment to *thrive with others,* including those who may not be in the same season or stage of life as you.

Life was designed to be a communal enterprise. Whether you're an extrovert or introvert, people oriented or task oriented, a coffee drinker or a tea drinker, a morning person or a night owl, God designed you to live in relationship with others.

This will require being attentive to what season those closest to you—whether it's your spouse, children, friends, or colleagues—are currently experiencing. Be aware of how they tend to behave in each season.

Keep in mind that God created a lot of people who are different than you. In fact, if you aren't careful, that can become a real problem.

The individuals around you may be in a different stage or season than you, so their outlook on life will be dissimilar from yours. The dichotomy can be either a source of conflict or a fabulous opportunity.

If you become irritated with people who don't view life the way *you* do, prepare to perpetually experience conflicts. On the other hand, just as the Creator delights in diversity, so people offer you potentially rich deposits of joy. The key is to be open to experiencing life from a multiplicity of angles and perspectives. Then spend time with people and see what happens.

It could be that you're in an autumn season, enjoying the fruits of your labors, while your spouse is in winter, seeing a stage of life drawing to a close. Or maybe you're swamped with summer responsibilities, while your daughter is enthralled with spring possibilities—a new school, job, and boyfriend. Make a list of people you relate to closely, and identify which season they currently occupy. Could that explain their current behavior? Could it shed light on conflicts you may have experienced recently? Understanding which season your friends, colleagues, and family members are in will help you to better understand, relate to, and enjoy them.

Let me share some practical suggestions with you at this point. I hear a lot of people bemoaning the fact they don't have anything in common with their spouse or child or colleague. Often after couples have divorced, they'll acknowledge that they shared no common interests—the wife was into jogging, gardening, and gourmet cooking, while her husband was into watching football all weekend. This is why I plead with young couples considering marriage to determine if there's anything beyond animal attraction that will hold them together five years from now.

As we've seen, couples can be in different seasons. One might be enmeshed in the summer of caring for preschoolers, while the other is experiencing the spring excitement of a new job. Or the wife may be at the peak of her profession, while winter has set in on her husband's career and he's now grappling with retirement. How do two people in different seasons thrive, together? If you're married, strive to find things that you and your spouse could enjoy doing together.

Lisa and I may be as polar opposite as two people can be and still live in the same galaxy. The list of our differences is long and emphatic.

She was brought up with six sisters and one brother. I had three brothers and one sister.

She's an off-the-chart feeler. I'm not emotive. In fact, Lisa questioned whether I even *had* feelings for the first decade of our marriage.

I grew up heavily involved in sports and was a fierce competitor. Lisa never played sports and is stricken with guilt and remorse if she actually beats someone in a competition.

I spent my early childhood in Los Angeles. She grew up in an isolated Canadian prairie town of a thousand people (although it boasted the most grain elevators per capita of any town in the province).

I'm a long-term thinker. To Lisa, long-range planning is deciding what to do after breakfast.

I'm an author and public speaker who travels every week and routinely mixes and mingles with the public. Lisa is a homebody who would rather be slowly lowered into a pool of molten lava than stand on a stage and talk into a microphone.

And so forth. With all these differences, we've experienced more than a few challenges in finding ways to enjoy life together, as you can well imagine. But we have managed to do so. After our first (and only) tennis match on our honeymoon, we concluded that head-to-head sporting competitions would not enhance our marital bliss. We've endeavored to find other things we could do to make life together a lot of fun.

For example, Lisa loves words. That has made her an excellent editor and also the Michael Jordan of the Scrabble world. So we play Scrabble. Since I travel a lot, we have two online games going continually, which has been great for staying in touch when I'm on the road. We got so carried away with it last Valentine's Day that our daughter found us in separate rooms of our house, fervently playing online Scrabble! (That drew my daughter's patented roll of her pretty eyes.)

We don't rappel off precipices or go whitewater rafting together, but we have fun in a quirky, literary sort of way. We also enjoy evening walks.

Some of our pastimes, such as shopping, are pure compromise. Lisa loves to shop. And me? Well, about that molten lava... But I do enjoy reading and drinking good coffee. So book in hand, I establish the base camp at a coffee shop in the mall, and Lisa periodically drops off her purchases before forging back into the jungle.

Couples can always find activities that bring them joy *together*, if they'll look hard enough.

And when children come along, a whole new avenue of possibilities opens up. That's what I want to explore with you next, in some detail… and with lots of fun.

REFLECT AND RESPOND

1. How strong is your commitment to *thrive* and not just survive? Is this truly a compelling pursuit in your life?

2. Are you in any way agitated or discouraged about your current situation in life? If so, what can you do to be more accepting of this situation and to thrive in it?

3. Who are the people you most want to partner with as you pursue your commitment to thrive in life? Do these people know and share your commitment?

4. How high is your joy threshold? Does it take very much for you to lose your joy? What kinds of experiences have caused you to lose your joy recently?

5. What is preventing you from having more joy in your life? What do you intend to do about that?

28

With Joy Comes Laughter

We've talked about the larger commitment to joy that's the secret to finding fulfillment in every season of life. In this chapter I want to get very specific about what this could look like in your home.

And it all starts with attitude.

Have you noticed that some people are no fun to be around? And do you know what's one of the most frequently used statuses on Facebook? "I'm *so* bored!" Don't get me started on that one. Let me just say this: if you're continually bored, then more than likely you have a dull life. And (to get really personal) you're probably a dull person.

The truth is, *exciting people have exciting lives.* They don't sit at home waiting for someone to call them up and rescue them from their lethargy.

Dreary people may wonder why they didn't get invited to the party or why their adult children never come home to visit. Many such people were never helped as children to learn how to be joy-producing people. Their parents were joyless, so they produced boring children. Now those children have grown up to become tedious adults who are rearing their own dull offspring. I'm not saying this to be overly critical. It's just an observation.

I know young singles who won't agree to attend a social function until they first learn who's coming, the schedule of activities, and the menu. Yet these same people contribute little to the festivities when present, and they seldom host enjoyable gatherings themselves. We've all known couples who never invite people to their home but are offended when no one extends an invitation to them. There are grandparents who take pride in not putting away their valuable artifacts when their grandchildren come to visit. But when the cherubs descend upon them for the holidays, the frazzled couple continually shouts, "Don't touch that!" while lecturing their bewildered toddlers on treating the property of others with due respect. They later wonder why the younger generation is always too busy to visit.

LAUGHTER AT HOME

People who were never helped to understand what a joyful home or life really looks like often don't have one.

Lisa and I both come from large, fun families. We decided early in our marriage that we wanted to produce a home of joy. It wasn't simply because that's the kind of home we wanted to experience ourselves but also because we wanted to teach our children how to be joyful people.

So here's our family: a busy father who travels for a living, a mom who often functions as a single parent, two sons who are quite different from each other, plus a princess. How do we all cohabitate so we don't just survive but thrive? It takes a lot of time, work, and planning (and ideally more than one bathroom).

And, by golly, we were successful. Ask my sons or daughter what it was like growing up in our home. They'll undoubtedly begin their answers by making a snide comment about my spending more time around flight attendants than my children, and they'll perhaps throw in a reference to the foreign languages spoken by their mother after she stubs her toe. But then they'll affirm that growing up in our home was a blast. We're not experts on marriage or family, but when it came to having a joyful home, we managed to get it right (most of the time).

Let me share some things we did to enable our home to regularly reverberate with laughter.

There were at least three major areas of our family life that we felt could provide reservoirs of happiness. Let me get real practical here and share some specific things we did. I don't mean to suggest you should do exactly the same things. This is merely to encourage you to make your home a place that your friends, children, and grandchildren love to visit. What we did worked for a family with two parents and three kids. You may be single or widowed or married without children or even great-grandparents. Everyone's situation is different, and so is the cash flow. It's certainly easier to orchestrate fun parties when you have the money to do it. But I also found that some of our most creative and memorable family times occurred when we were operating on a tight budget, which was most of the time.

Here's the point: are you being intentional about making your home a place people like to be?

Laughter in Everyday Life

What makes good homes great? It's when ordinary events and objects are transformed into the extraordinary. People can't wait until their birthdays or the company Christmas party every year before they have a good time!

Let me give you an example. Beside our front door we have two stone statues of lions that we found in a yard sale. The one on the right is named Winston. The one on the left isn't.

Lots of houses have decorations of some sort; that's ordinary. But Lisa dresses these lions up according to the season or current activity in our home. They could be sporting summer hats and sunglasses or psychedelic hippie outfits or umbrellas or graduation caps. During winter they may be wrapped cozily in knit scarves or showing off their Santa hats.

We have cars and people on bikes regularly stopping by our house to see Winston's latest attire. A woman who lives a thousand miles away was so delighted with the changing costumes on our lions she saw posted on Facebook that she made an entire pictorial album of our lions and mailed it to us.

Okay, you may be thinking, *Dressing up your stone lions sounds strange.* Yes, but it makes our house a little more magical than houses whose stone statues look perfect year in and year out.

We also chose to outfit our home with supplies that could bring joy at a moment's notice. If you don't have a chocolate fountain, consider purchasing one. They aren't expensive, but they can turn mundane evenings into a gala event. (Chocolate could make an IRS audit fun!) It always amazes us how grown adults turn into giggling partiers when they get to dip their fruit into flowing chocolate!

Borrowing an idea from Lisa's sister (we borrow *lots* of ideas), we built up a costume closet. (You can do the same; just go to a Goodwill store or your parents' clothes closet to get started.) Over the years we've held parties where the dress-up theme was black and white, western, Disney, hillbilly, nerd, and Hollywood. Kids love to dress up—at all ages!

Once, on extremely short notice, our son Mike needed an evening activity for the college group he was leading. We had about an hour to prepare for two dozen guests. We raided the costume closet and assigned character roles to each guest. After they arrived and were dressed up, we grabbed the video camera and made a hilarious film in which every person played a part. One young man in the group was legally blind. He donned a tablecloth, knelt on all fours, and stuck a fruit basket on his back. He was the table in the movie! He talked about his "starring" role for months afterward. Frankly, I thought his performance was a little flat.

One thing we found in having costume parties was that our kids learned not to take themselves too seriously. It's an invaluable trait to be able to take some good-natured ribbing (like the time our teenage boys dressed as Pocahontas and Captain John Smith). It was never just about looking silly.

When our kids were young, we'd try to change our normal routine now and then. One evening everyone in the family came to the dinner table dressed and acting like someone else in the family. The meal was hilarious (and starkly revealing of how our kids viewed their parents). On St. Patrick's Day all the food was dyed green. On the last day of school, Lisa threw a beach party (we were eight hundred miles from an ocean and nowhere near a swimming pool). Another year we held our own Olympics.

My children always loved to make homemade movies. When my ninety-year-old grandfather came to visit, we enlisted him in a swash-buckling tale of pirates on the high seas. Tragically, however, dear old grandpa was dragged from the ship to a watery grave by an enormous tentacle that looked eerily like a Hoover vacuum hose.

The key was to do something different and put a twist on ordinary events so we had a new excuse for laughter. Our children never knew what to expect, so living in our home was an adventure. And they learned that transforming the ordinary into the extraordinary allows people of every age to enjoy life together in surprising ways.

LAUGHTER IN SPECIAL EVENTS

A second springboard to tons of fun in our family was our approach to special events. When Lisa threw a party, the entire house was trans-formed.

For our Hollywood party she found a red carpet that ran out to the street and a fake palm tree replete with paparazzi leaping out from behind it to take pictures as guests disembarked from their valet-parked vehicles. Our house has undergone a metamorphosis into an enchanted forest in which everything green we owned was dragged into the living room. There were fake birds (including sounds of chirping), bunnies, and gnomes. Our home has also been the backdrop for a hillbilly hoedown, a hippie commune, a punk party, a truck stop, a silent movie set, and a town out of the Wild West.

All of this took a lot of work, but, boy, did we make memories! For some of these events we purchased a few accessories, but most of them were built around clothes or props we'd collected over the years. (Sadly, many of the costumes people used for the nerd party came out of my active wardrobe.) Often we would ask our nieces or friends of our children to come over early and help decorate. That was usually as much fun as the party.

Much of the success of these events lay in involving all generations in the festivities. For example, at the Hollywood party, people were divided into teams and assigned a theme or a prop or names of fictional characters, then given ten minutes to come up with a scene in which *everyone* had to act. The kids laughed themselves silly watching their parents acting crazy and being great sports. The oldest generation (the grandparents in attendance) served as the panel of judges to award the prizes (fake Oscar trophies that Lisa found online) to the winners of each category. Besides being a fun party, it allowed grandparents, parents, and teenage kids to all laugh together. The fun reached across the generations. Imagine my revered father judging the "artistic" merit of my son Daniel's impersonation of a female rock star. Or when Phyllis, my long-tenured administrative assistant, and her husband, Ross—both in their sixties—whacked at hockey pucks in our garage in order to win a small plastic trophy.

It truly is rewarding when two or three different generations laugh together under the same roof.

LAUGHTER ON BIRTHDAYS

A regular occurrence that naturally lends itself to fostering joy is, of course, a birthday party. I know some frazzled parents who feel lucky just getting a cake baked or bought in time. But we always put a lot of work into these events because we felt it was a great opportunity to build up our kids and to have fun as a family. Lisa would plan months in advance to ensure that she had all the necessary props and supplies.

We gave Carrie an *I Love Lucy* party one year in which all the girls came dressed as Lucy. Then they acted out famous scenes (such as the chocolate conveyer belt), which we filmed and replayed on the television.

Carrie's favorite party had an *Amazing Race* theme, and teams raced all over town to find clues and do hilarious exercises. To be safe, each team was driven by an amiable (and responsible) parent. We gave each team a CD containing various songs, with each tune providing the clue to the next destination. "Paperback Writer" by the Beatles sent them racing to the local bookstore. The theme to *Chariots of Fire* directed them to the indoor running track. At each destination, a store manager or receptionist would hand them instructions that had to be followed to the letter before they could move on.

One stop was at Guy's Bakery and Sandwich Shop. When the girls arrived, the proprietor (aptly named Guy) lined up a row of chairs in the middle of his crowded restaurant and had the girls stand on them and perform a song (in the form of a round) before they could leave. The patrons applauded, and off the girls went.

At another stop the kids were handed a bag of plastic instruments and told to play music outside the store until they received a donation. Eventually a patron dropped a coin in their bucket just to make them stop.

One of my daughter's favorite birthday party rituals was "story time." I would assign every person a role, they would put on the appropriate costume, and then I would tell a story. Whenever I mentioned a character in the tale, the participants would act out the events. Of course the birthday girl was always the beautiful princess while her brothers and cousin were perennially consigned to be bad guys who were ultimately foiled and beaten up by the magical creatures and fair maidens. We would film the play, then sit and watch the finished production together. Even years later I'd run into girls in our community who would excitedly reminisce about the creatures and heroines they'd played over the years at Carrie's birthday parties.

DON'T SETTLE FOR BLAND

Why do I share these stories? Not to impress you but to inspire you. Too many people settle for bland, ordinary, or, worse yet, boring living rather than the fulfilling, joyful life God created them to experience. Lisa and I not only wanted our children to have a blast while growing up, but we also wanted them to learn how to *be* fun people. We tried to instill in them a sense of humor (although they never became fond of my puns, despite my heroic efforts). Today our kids know how to have fun, and they're the kind of people you'd want to invite to your party. But more important than the parties are the people skills they learned: hospitality, thoughtfulness, planning, gratitude, and humility, to name a few. Those are invaluable skills for every season of a person's life.

Perhaps you grew up in a family like mine; we didn't have much money or square footage in our house, but there was a lot of laughter. Or maybe there wasn't much levity in your home, and as a result perhaps it doesn't come naturally to you. The truth is, regardless of your upbringing, God wants you to live with joy. People express it differently. My wife laughs until she falls to the ground. My daughter is famous for her "seal" laugh, which results from inhaling so deeply she can't breathe. I have a friend who gets hysterical by raising one eyebrow higher than the other.

The culmination of all the parties and good times is what we call "lore." Those are the memories of the crazy things family and friends said and did that made us laugh and that symbolized their unique personalities. There is lore from all the uncles and aunts as well as cousins. Lisa has recorded the most humorous things our family has said and done over the years. Now many years later we still laugh uproariously when she pulls out the book and we recall the great times of the past.

This is what I wish for you: that you and your family would steadily and often collect your own family lore that you and your loved ones will still be chuckling over many years from now. They'll be treasured markers and milestones commemorating all the seasons of your life together.

REFLECT AND RESPOND

1. Are you the kind of person who brings joy to others? Are you enjoyable to be around? How does bringing joy to others affect your own level of joy?

2. Do you laugh often? Would other people around you say that they often hear you laugh?

3. What's one thing you could do to transform something ordinary in your home into something extraordinary?

4. What's the most enjoyable party you ever held or attended? Why was it so much fun? Would it be possible to do something similar to that again?

5. What's one thing you could do to create a special event in the life of others? What's one thing you could do to make someone's birthday extra special?

29

Reclaiming Lost Seasons

As we approach the end of our journey here together, I suspect I've only begun to uncover the manifold implications for our lives that derive from the seasons. Nevertheless, I hope the truths we've touched on in these pages have accomplished for you what they have for me—inspiring you, stretching your thinking, and challenging you.

I trust that seeing your life more clearly in terms of seasonal cycles has given you some fresh perspectives. Perhaps you have a firmer grasp on your current situation and more clarity regarding your past. Since seasons come in a predictable order, you can also have a better sense of what's coming next.

But more than seeing your life through a new metaphorical lens, I hope you've been encouraged to live a life that truly thrives, one that constantly capitalizes on God-given joy.

Let me urge you again to *strive* for this joy—not just for your own sake but also for others in your life, such as your spouse, friends, colleagues, and especially your children. It's the only life you'll ever have. And no one can live it for you. It matters not if you have a thousand excuses for why your life isn't joyful. At the end of the day, it's far better to have a good life than a good excuse!

But still, excuses come easily for us, especially in light of the many challenges we all face in life.

During—and After—the Storms

Several years ago Lisa and I bought a house in a relatively new neighborhood. We moved in on a day in February when the temperature plunged to forty below zero.

We loved the house. The yard, however, was shrouded in mystery. It was covered in snow, so we had no idea what it would look like after the spring thaw. We hoped the previous owners were skilled horticulturalists and that, come spring, our surroundings would burst forth with bountiful flowers, verdant grass, and luscious foliage.

Spring came. No foliage. Not even a stray tulip. We stared out our window at a barren wasteland.

To make things worse, it turned out that all our neighbors were avid (dare I say fanatical?) gardeners. Every yard on our block showed evidence of tender nurturing. You see, in most of Canada the growing season for flowers is brief, lasting only from mid-June until mid-September. After a bitterly long, cold winter, Canadians become zealous about their yards. Many of our neighbors spent every evening on their hands and knees gently coddling their little plants, trimming their hedges, fertilizing their delicate blossoms, and talking softly to their most prized vegetation. But walking through our yard reminded me of the first lunar landing—nary a sign of life!

We had to do something fast, or we would be the disgrace of the neighborhood.

Lisa and I hastened to the nearest gardening store. We bought bedding plants, tools, fertilizer, and dirt. (I'd never paid hard-earned money for dirt before, but these were desperate times.) We built a gorgeous flower mound in our front yard. We planted shrubs, perennials, and annuals. Every day Lisa fertilized, deadheaded old buds, and weeded the flowers. We rejoiced over every new blossom.

One day I arrived home from work and noticed Lisa standing outside, admiring her handiwork on our flower mound. The blooms were spectacular! I stepped beside her, and we celebrated our phenomenal success.

A woman walking her dog stopped and personally *thanked* us, on behalf of the neighborhood, for beautifying what was formerly an unpopular eyesore on our street. Meanwhile the local newspaper listed our house in a column citing the most beautiful yards in town that summer. We were elated! This was a triumph of Olympian proportions!

That evening as we sat at the dinner table, we heard a strange sound that gradually grew louder. *Ping...ping...ping...* As I rose to investigate, the noise intensified. I opened the front door to witness the worst hailstorm in our town's history (virtually every roof in our neighborhood would need its shingles replaced). I gasped to see huge hailstones pulverizing our precious plants. Small branches were severed from the trees and littered our lawn.

I heard Lisa scream as she raced onto our veranda to join me. Horrified, she uttered those desperate words husbands have dreaded for millennia: "Don't just stand there. DO SOMETHING!"

In desperation I surveyed the white mass of icy projectiles roaring downward, pummeling our defenseless vegetation. At that moment my manhood was in jeopardy. I was the hunter and gatherer for my family, my home's defender. I entertained the desperate notion of racing through the maelstrom to the flower mound and flinging my body across it, sacrificing my mortal flesh for whatever plants I might snatch from ruin. But as quickly as it began, the storm subsided.

The carnage was pitiful. Neighbors somberly trudged out to survey the damage. Some were in tears. A midsummer hailstorm had rocked our world.

Fortunately for us, we lost only flowers, which in Canada have a briefer life span than a New Year's resolution. It's far more serious, however, when unexpected storms deluge your life. You may have been reading this book and thinking, *My life has been a horror story, not a fairy tale.* You might have been building a comfortable, pleasant existence when ominous storm clouds suddenly appeared. Perhaps you discovered your spouse was having an affair, and now you abruptly find yourself a single parent. Maybe you've suffered the loss of a child. You might have been downsized at work or suffered betrayal from someone you trusted, and now your dreams of financial security have degenerated into a nightmare. You may have made serious mistakes in judgment that are now costing you dearly. Perhaps you gravely mishandled a season or two, and now your life is dreary and devoid of satisfaction. Maybe you rushed your spring or were careless in summer, and now your autumn is barren. As we've seen, seasons have their dark side.

If you wish you could turn your life around or reclaim lost seasons in your life, let me offer you hope. Remember most of all that *God always has another spring awaiting you.* We cannot go back and change the past no matter how desperately we wish we could. But we can embrace the next spring that comes.

I know numerous people who made foolish and costly mistakes in the past. They would do anything to erase that portion of their lives along with the painful consequences that ensued. But they can't. Nonetheless, though God seldom removes the consequences of our earlier decisions, He does bring new spring seasons to our lives and helps us to make healthy choices next time.

Some people make mistakes in their marriage relationship that result in divorce. Eventually these people may gain a lucid perspective on their lives and realize how their behavior contributed to the dissolution of their marriages. Clearly it's too late to go back and change the past. But that certainly doesn't mean their lives are over or that they're without possibilities.

Spring doesn't provide identical opportunities to everyone, but when opportunities come, people must seize what God offers. Recently I met a couple whose marriage succumbed to divorce several years earlier. They went their separate ways. Four years later neither had remarried, and they had found their way back into different churches. That fall both churches offered a study of the course *Experiencing God*. Unbeknownst to each other, they both enrolled in the study and were deeply impacted by the experience.

Through the material God revealed to both of them that they had been selfish and inflexible in their relationship and that their marriage need not have ended. One day they met for coffee, each desiring to apologize to the other for contributing to their marriage's demise. Ultimately they remarried.

When I met them, they'd been happily remarried for three years. A new spring provided them the opportunity to try marriage to each other a second time, and this time they got it right.

You may have mishandled your last season of life, but God's presence is still available to you today. You may be in winter and watching a stage of your life draw to a close, yet you can still have joy. You may be in the frenetically busy summer season, yet in the midst of your hectic schedule, you can still thrive. You may have just had a hailstorm decimate the flowers in your front yard, but you can still have an abundant life!

YES, THERE IS HOPE

I've been inspired by the story of Nell Kerley. For the first sixty-six years of her life, Nell regularly attended church and was a typical North American Christian. Then one day she and her husband were involved in a horrific car accident. Nell suffered multiple broken bones and experienced unbearable pain. In her agony Nell cried out to God, "Take me home!" In answer she sensed God telling her, *I am not done with you yet.*

She and her husband endured a lengthy recuperation in the hospital. As a result of her extensive injuries, Nell underwent seventeen surgeries. Today she suffers from diabetes, arthritis, and non-Hodgkin's lymphoma. She has no kneecaps and has screws holding her ankles in place.

In 1998, at age sixty-six, Nell heard of a class at her church that taught people how to share their faith with others. Though she was easily the oldest person taking the course, Nell sensed that God wanted her to share the gospel with as many people as she could in the remaining time God granted her. At the close of the class, Nell's instructor gave her the opportunity to share her faith with someone who was not a Christian. To Nell's amazement, the person prayed with her to accept Christ into her life. Nell was hooked!

That was fourteen years ago. I talked with Nell recently and asked her how many people she has led to faith in Christ since that first time. As of our phone call, she was up to 3,142! And she's still going strong.

Nell had been a typical church attendee for the first six decades of her life. Today she's a fireball. She's a regular guest in evangelism classes at Liberty University, she's having an enormous impact on others, and her life is filled with joy.[38]

Regardless of what your life has been like in the past, you're always one spring away from a whole new life of meaning and fulfillment.

There are innumerable past mistakes that can potentially prevent you from experiencing joy today. Perhaps you dropped out of college and have hated your subsequent jobs ever since. You may have made an ill-advised investment. Maybe your children are struggling in their lives, and you feel remorse over the way you parented them. It's impossible to list all the ways people limit their lives through unhealthy choices. Nevertheless, there is hope. Forgetting what lies behind, as the apostle Paul claimed, we can press on to the next opportunity God provides (Philippians 3:13–14).

The message of the gospel is that regardless of what mistakes or tragedies or failures or neglect you've experienced in the past, God has an infinite number of springtimes at His disposal, and any one of them can forever change your life.

I have in my office a framed, hand-drawn picture of the face of Jesus. Interwoven throughout the drawing are various scenes from the life of Christ. What makes this picture so special is not just that it's beautifully done but that it represents a new spring in someone's life.

The artist grew up in an unbelievably harsh and abusive home. To survive, she developed a fierce demeanor and a violent temper. She was ultimately consigned for the remainder of her life to a maximum security prison in Louisiana.

This woman hadn't chosen the dysfunctional family into which she was born, nor had she asked for the abuse that had been heaped upon her. Nevertheless, her response to her circumstances meant she would spend the remainder of her unhappy life in prison, without friends or family or hope.

Or would she?

When I spoke to the prison chaplain about this woman, he described her as the "meanest person" he'd ever met. Even the guards were afraid of her. But then she experienced a life-transforming encounter with Christ. God brought healing to her broken and disillusioned heart. She experienced joy as well as genuine friendships for the first time.

Then she discovered art. She'd never drawn anything before. She found she had a knack for doing landscapes and also portraits of Jesus. She painted some spectacular murals in the prison chapel and in the chaplain's office.

As my father and I completed a conference at the prison, she presented each of us with a beautiful picture she'd drawn of Jesus. She was amazed that Christ had never given up on her, had found her in prison, and had given her the skill to create works of art.

While this woman is unlikely to ever leave prison, she experienced a new spring there, and as a result today she's creating things that are beautiful. And she has joy.

In every stage of life, it's possible to reclaim lost seasons. Life might not turn out the way we always dreamed, but it can still be amazing!

Let God show you what changes you need to make in your viewpoint, attitude, and behaviors. God designed you to live life abundantly. He can show you how to do it, and He can provide you every resource necessary to make it happen. I wish you God's very best in your efforts.

As you move forward from season to season, rest in God's forgiveness of your past mistakes, and press on to the abundant life He has for you in the future.

God has countless amazing experiences in His warehouse to offer you. His mercies and compassion are "*new* every morning" (Lamentations 3:22–23). On the basis of such overflowing grace from our loving Father, I pray that He'll do a fresh, new work in your life…and bring your way what He long ago promised His people: "seasons of joy and gladness and cheerful feasts" (Zechariah 8:19, ESV).

REFLECT AND RESPOND

1. What past storms in your life have most affected your outlook about living a joyful life?

2. What is *one* thing you could do right away to more fully and joyfully trust God in the seasons of your life still to come?

3. How would you describe your strongest hope for the future?

4. How has reading this book helped you most?

5. What further questions have been raised in your mind and heart from reading this book?

NOTES

1. Derek Kidner, *The Message of Ecclesiastes,* The Bible Speaks Today (Downers Grove, IL: InterVarsity, 1976), 37–38.

2. Iain Provan, *Ecclesiastes, Song of Songs,* The NIV Application Commentary (Grand Rapids, MI: Zondervan, 2001), 87.

3. Provan, *Ecclesiastes,* 87.

4. Provan, *Ecclesiastes,* 88.

5. Provan, *Ecclesiastes,* 88.

6. Provan, *Ecclesiastes,* 89.

7. Kidner, *The Message of Ecclesiastes,* 38–39.

8. Lewis Carroll, *Alice's Adventures in Wonderland; Through the Looking-Glass* (1866; repr., London: Macmillan, 1920), 89.

9. Lisa Watson, "Girl's Legacy Continues After Cancer Battle," *Arkansas Baptist News,* October 7, 2010, 12.

10. Peter Arnell, *Shift: How to Reinvent Your Business, Your Career, and Your Personal Brand* (New York: Crown Business, 2010).

11. Malcolm Gladwell, *Outliers: The Story of Success* (New York: Little, Brown, 2008), 73ff.

12. Gladwell, *Outliers,* 111–12.

13. Wes Moore, *The Other Wes Moore: One Name, Two Fates* (New York: Spiegel and Grau, 2011).

14. Howard Gardner, *Multiple Intelligences: New Horizons in Theory and Practice,* rev. ed. (New York: Basic Books, 2006).

15. Walter Isaacson, *Einstein: His Life and His Universe* (New York: Simon and Schuster, 2007), 439.

16. Daniel Goleman, *Working with Emotional Intelligence* (New York: Bantam Books, 2000), 5.

17. Richard Blackaby, *Unlimiting God: Increasing Your Capacity to Experience the Divine* (Colorado Springs: Multnomah, 2008).

18. Mike and Daniel Blackaby, *When Worlds Collide: Stepping Up and Standing Out in an Anti-God Culture* (Nashville: B and H Books, 2011).

19. Seth Godin, *Tribes: We Need You to Lead Us* (New York: Portfolio, 2008), 101.

20. You can read his story in Dennis Shere, *Cain's Redemption: A Story of Hope and Transformation in America's Bloodiest Prison* (Chicago: Northfield, 2005).

21. Seth Godin, *Linchpin: Are You Indispensable?* (New York: Portfolio, 2010).

22. Doris Kearns Goodwin wrote a popular study of Lincoln in office titled *Team of Rivals: The Political Genius of Abraham Lincoln* (New York: Simon and Schuster, 2005). My favorite biography of Churchill is by William Manchester, *The Last Lion*, 2 vols. (New York: Dell, 1983–88).

23. Alison Weir, *Elizabeth the Queen* (London: Jonathan Cape, 1998).

24. Joyce Bedi, "Edison Invents!" The Lemelson Center, http://invention.smithsonian.org/centerpieces/edison/000_story_02.asp.

25. Neil Baldwin, *Edison: Inventing the Century* (Chicago: University of Chicago Press, 2001), 355.

26. Eric Metaxas, *Amazing Grace: William Wilberforce and the Heroic Campaign to End Slavery* (San Francisco: HarperCollins, 2007).

27. It may be found in both workbook and trade book form. See Henry and Richard Blackaby, Claude King, *Experiencing God: Knowing and Doing the Will of God*, rev. ed. (Nashville: B and H Books, 2008).

28. Ron Powers, *Mark Twain: A Life* (New York: Free Press, 2006), 493.

29. H. W. Brands, *T.R.: The Last Romantic* (New York: Basic Books, 1997), 535.

30. J. Oswald Sanders, *Spiritual Leadership* (Chicago: Moody Press, 1980), 232.

31. David Cannadine, *Mellon: An American Life* (New York: Vintage Books, 2008), 189.

32. Ron Chernow, *Titan: The Life of John D. Rockefeller, Sr.* (New York: Vintage Books, 2004), 623–24.

33. Cannadine, *Mellon,* 574.

34. Janice Hudson, *Trauma Junkie: Memoirs of an Emergency Flight Nurse,* rev. ed. (Buffalo: Firefly Books, 2010), 223.

35. Charles Spurgeon, *Joy in Christ's Presence* (New Kensington, PA: Whitaker, 1997), 12, 29.

36. "Fauja Singh Becomes Oldest Marathon Runner," *BBC News: US and Canada,* October 16, 2011, www.bbc.co.uk/news/world-us-canada-15330421.

37. Blackaby, *Unlimiting God,* 127–46.

38. Polly House, "2,000 and Counting: Soul Winner Still Going Strong," *Baptist Courier,* September, 17, 2007, www.baptist courier.com/1926.article.

Allow God's mighty power
to infuse every area of your life!

More books by
RICHARD BLACKABY

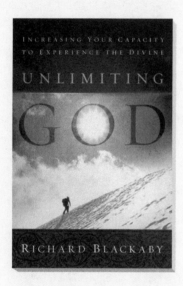

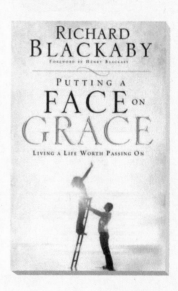

Find out more information and read an excerpt from these books on WaterBrookMultnomah.com!

ADDITIONAL BLACKABY RESOURCES

Experience more of God's power through these Blackaby ministry resources.

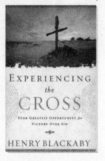 

 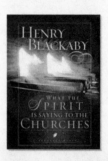

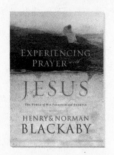  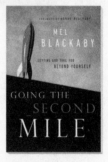

For more information visit WaterBrookMultnomah.com!